TAUBADA TIME

PAPUA NEW GUINEA

NOEL TUNNY

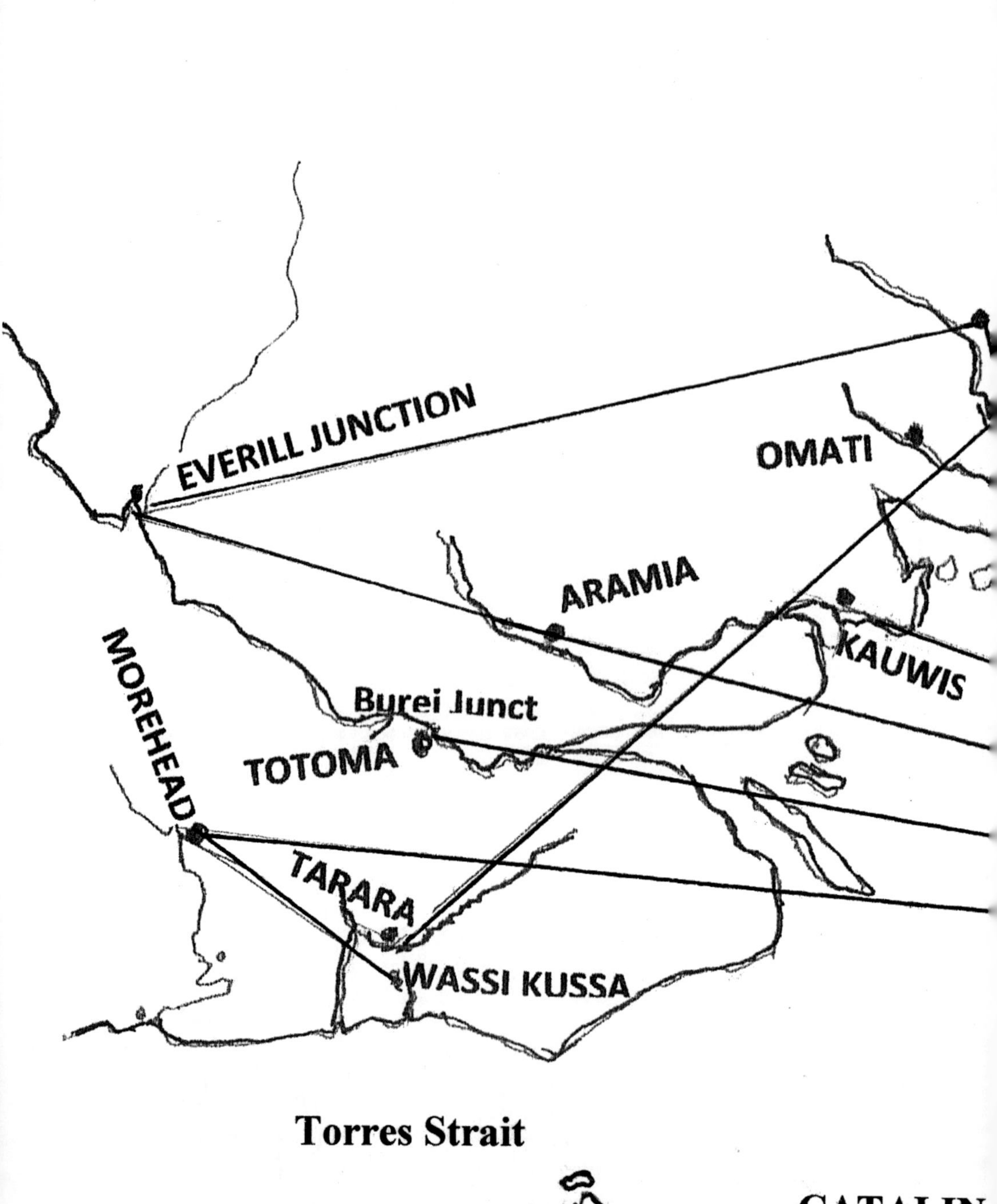
EVERILL JUNCTION
OMATI
ARAMIA
KAUWIS
MOREHEAD
Burei Junct
TOTOMA
TARARA
WASSI KUSSA
Torres Strait
CATALIN
Qld

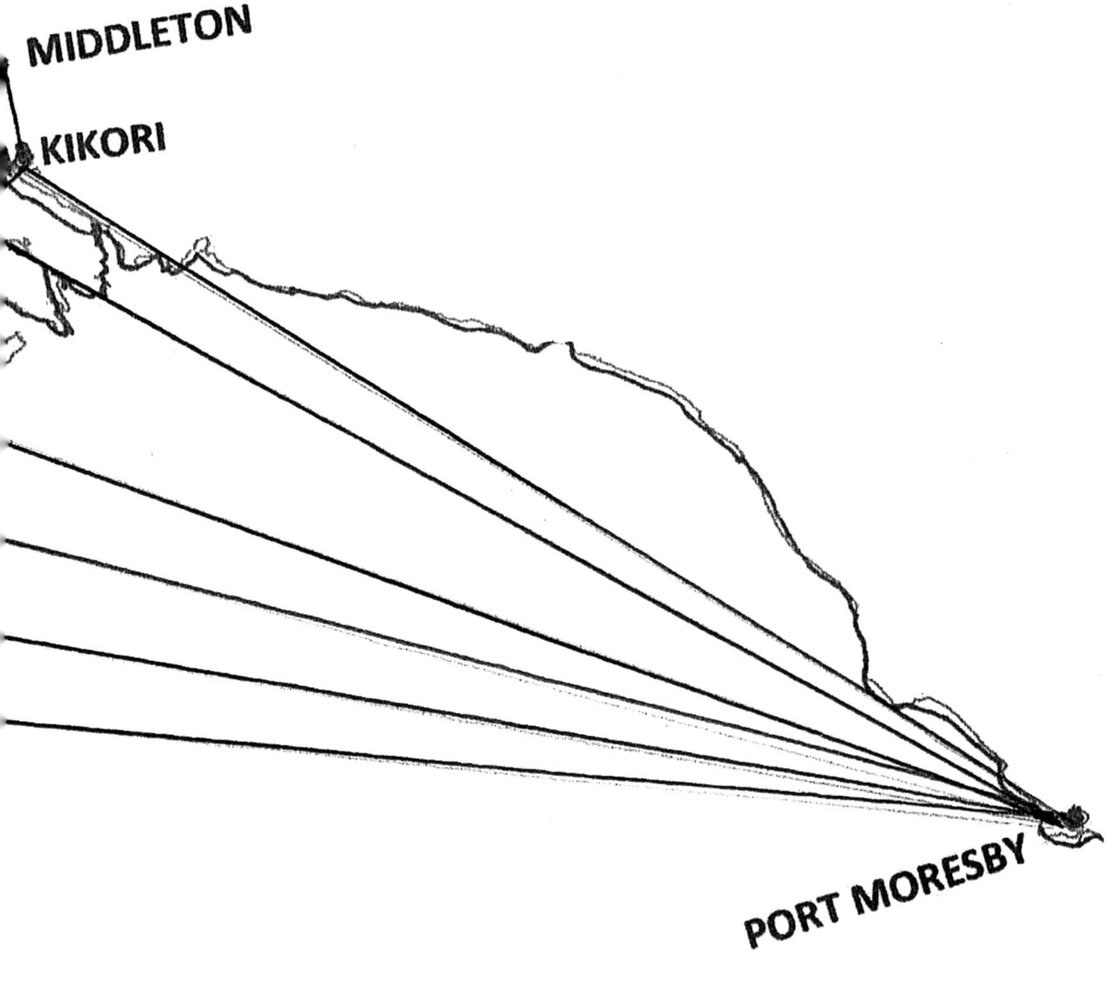

MIDDLETON

KIKORI

PORT MORESBY

TRAVEL RECORD

First published 2014

National Library of Australia Cataloguing-in-Publication entry:

Author:	Tunny, Noel, author.
Title:	Taubada time Papua New Guinea / Noel Tunny.
ISBN:	9781925046526 (paperback)
Subjects:	Tunny, Noel.
	Australasian Petroleum Company.
	Surveyors--Australia--Biography.
	Surveying--Papua New Guinea.
	Petroleum--Prospecting Petroleum--Papua New Guinea.
	Papua New Guinea--Description and travel.
Dewey Number:	622.1828092

Typeset in Paramount 13pt.

Cover Design: Boolarong Press

Cover Images: Paradisaea Rubra (Red Bird of Paradise)

All photographs unless stated are sourced from author.

Published by Boolarong Press, Salisbury, Brisbane, Australia.

Printed and bound by Watson Ferguson & Company, Salisbury, Brisbane, Australia.

This book is dedicated to the memory of

Captain Edmund Henry Buckingham Baker D.S.O, RN.

and

Major Leslie Philip Bliaux, B.Sc. MM. MBE

Who both made significant contributions by their leadership in the search for oil in Papua New Guinea.

Foreword

Though we don't discuss it much in strategic debate in Australia these days, there is no piece of geography more critical to Australia than Papua New Guinea and on the other side, West Irian. There was once a premium of knowledge about the area. When I was involved in the student activity in the late 1960s, the Australian Union of Students had a Papua New Guinea Oficer. It was the focus of idealism, strategic and economic concern. While that has disappeared from public commentary, the significance of the country is still recognised by our bureaucracy. Our Embasy in PNG is bigger than the one I am responsible for in Washington.

Like many families of that generation my family had connections with Papua New Guinea. Apart from a father who visited, I had an uncle who worked with the Methodist Mission in Rabaul. He was lost in the tragic sinking of the Montevideo Maru whilst a Japanese prisoner. The histories of many engaged mid-century with Papua New Guinea throw light on our understanding of developmental issues in this vital part of the world for us. Noel Tunny has again done a service to us all with his writing and has made the era live.

When he went out alone on his first survey with his team of Papuans he did not know the language and had no experience of working with Papuans. Despite these shortcomings his trust and friendly leadership was rewarded with loyalty and performance beyond his expectations.

His personal experiences and the goodwill he enjoyed remind us of the debt of gratitude we owe to these same people who supported the soldiers at Kokoda and elsewhere in New Guinea during the WWII.

Read about some of the men who played a significant part in the search and discovery of oil and gas in Papua. These were important contributions in light of the fact that PNG is about to become one of the world's big suppliers of oil and gas. One of these men was Major Leslie Philip Bliaux a science graduate from the United Kingdom who had worked as a geophysicist on oil search in Persia before coming to New Guinea.Phil was parachuted with his battalion into Arnhem as a participant in the *Bridge Too Far* episode after D day during WWII.

Another was Captain Edwin Henry 'Buck' Baker, in 1953 Aide de Camp to Queen Elizabeth and former prisoner of war after his capture during a clandestine evacuation of troops from the occupied island Leros in the Aegean. Captain Baker was contracted to Australasian Petroleum Company to do hydrographic surveys of Papuan rivers likely to be used by large ships when production of oil began.

The surveys described in Taubada Time were done in the areas north and south of the Fly River that figures in all the major expeditions and explorations of Papua in from 1845 through to the 1930s.

The book has a summary of these adventures that tells the stories of the men and the ships involved. In 1954 Captain Baker did a survey of the Fly River 'in the wake' of another Royal Navy hydrographer Captain Francis Blackwood who discovered and named the Fly River in 1845.

Some skilled and experienced people came from across the globe to search for oil with the Australasian Petroleum Company. They used a full array of air and maritime capabilities and state of the art scientific kit in their search. However nothing would have been achieved were it not for the goodwill and cooperation of the mainly uneducated Papuans who in many cases became true friends of the taubadas.

No one is better suited to provide a literary setting for all of this than Noel Tunny. We are in his debt.

His Excellency The Honorable Kim Beazley, AC
Ambassador to United States of America

Contents

Preface

This book tells the story of a surveyor working in the bush for Australasian Petroleum Company at a time when that company was searching for oil in Papua in 1954.

I was that twenty three year old surveyor and while writing of my own experiences I realised the importance of the Fly River in the development of Papua. I decided that the stories of the men associated with that development should be told along with the account of my experiences in that same part of Papua.

When you go bush on your own with twenty young Papuans you soon learn that without their goodwill and support you are not able to do your job. I was accepted as part of their team although I was leading the survey. I hope that my recollection of their loyalty gives them the credit they deserve

In the 1950s the native Papuan New Guineans were starting to assume the leadership roles in administration and commerce. That evolution heralded the end of the taubadas and the emergence of the expatriates with their diminished authority.

In British New Guinea the Europeans who came as administrators, miners or plantation managers were generally taller than the locals and were known by their description in the motu language. tau being man and bada being big.

The areas surveyed are described in stories and illustrated by photographs. All areas adjoin the Fly River for some miles from its north bank and some miles from its south bank.

I describe my experiences, some unique, frankly and in detail so that you can know what can happen to you when you go bush in Papua New Guinea.

List of Photographs

About the Author

Joseph Noel Tunny, a retired consulting engineer, was born on the 13th of September 1930 at Mareeba, North Queensland. His father, Harry Tunny,was a railway station master.

Noel as he is known was educated at Mount Carmel College, Charters Towers and at the University of Queensland, Brisbane, gaining the degree of Bachelor of Engineering (Civil) 1955.

Final year engineering had to be done as a full-time student so to fund this requirement Noel took 1954 off from his studies and worked as an unlicensed surveyor in Papua.

Early work for the Australasian Petroleum Company involved setting out seismic survey lines in the bush areas near the Fly and the Aramia Rivers. This work was interrupted by a period spent on hydrographic survey with M.V. Tiveri

As a part time student in the second and third years of his course Noel had worked with the Queensland Irrigation and Rivers Department in the hydrographic section. This experience plus his having passed third year surveying probably explains why he was chosen to work on M.V. Tiveri, which vessel under Captain Edmund "Buck" Baker was then being used to survey and chart rivers in Papua for the Australasian Petroleum Company.

Author and Kiwai team leader Emalio on beachfront at Bula

Acknowledgements

Writing History necessitates becoming dependent on the work of others and upon the availability of the facts and detail needed to record what Sir George MacAulay Trevelyan described as "the impelling poetry of truth in historical study."

The computer with Wikipedia and others has simplified and speeded up the research, but the cooperation and the skill of the librarians is decisive.

Accordingly I record my thanks and gratitude to the many people and institutions that responded to my requests for information.

At the head of the list is Mrs Patricia Sheppard who is Captain Baker's daughter and our meeting is a joyful and sentimental memory.

Claire Cruickshank of the National Library of Australia tracked down the Colin Simpson article on Oil Search at Everill Junction in the second of March 1954 edition of the magazine "A.M." Revisiting this pivotal item spurred me on.

Joy Horton the manager of archives for Oil Search made it possible to get the detailed facts on base locations and survey records essential for real history.

Elizabeth Alvey, librarian at the University of Queensland's Fryer Library made available maps photographs and reports from the early seismic surveys that hopefully have added interest and fact to this record.

The original charts and plots of the early surveys by Captain Blackwood in HMS *Fly*, Luigi Maria D'Albertis in steam launch Neva and Captain Everill in S.S.Bonito were copied and supplied by the State Library of New South Wales.

A copy of the map drawn by J.B. Chambers detailing Sir Willliam MacGregor's voyage up the Fly and Palmer rivers was supplied by the Royal Geographic Society,London

The Royal Hydrographic Service at Taunton, Somerset, United Kingdom added to the service record of Captain Baker R.N.,

Again Phil Dougherty of Ed's PCs at Toowong, Brisbane eliminated all technical computer problems. Also I am indebted to my good friend Ian Harris who brought his training and experience as a solicitor with advice and general proof reading

Without all the above help writing this small history would have been impossible.

Chapter 1
Searching for Oil

By 1954 Australasian Petroleum Company (A.P.C.) had established a large field operation in Papua. A.P.C. scientists were searching for any geologic structures in Papua that might have trapped oil.

The scientists did this by using seismic and gravity survey techniques to plot likely structures deep in the earth. Deep drilling of any promising formations would later decide whether or not oil was present.

Seismic survey in the A.P.C. search for oil involved measuring the earth's properties by the physical principles of elasticity (seismic).

A.P.C. generated seismic waves by detonating dynamite in drill holes (shot points) and measuring the reflected and refracted waves with geophones positioned at known distances along the survey line. Each line would have eight geophones spaced 1,200 feet apart making three and a half miles of line for each shot point.

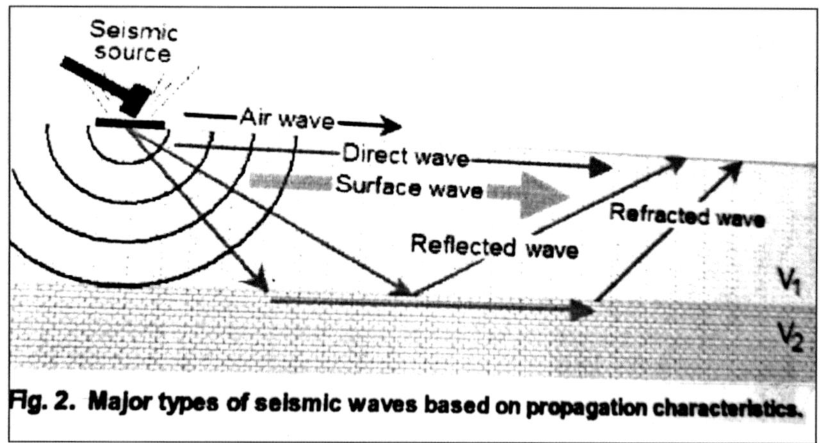

Fig. 2. Major types of seismic waves based on propagation characteristics.

Seismic Waves Diagram

Source: Wikipedia

The surveyors located the shot points and the geophone stations and marked them for future identification by he field geophysicists.

Gravity survey measures the differences in the force of gravity at different points along a gravity survey line.

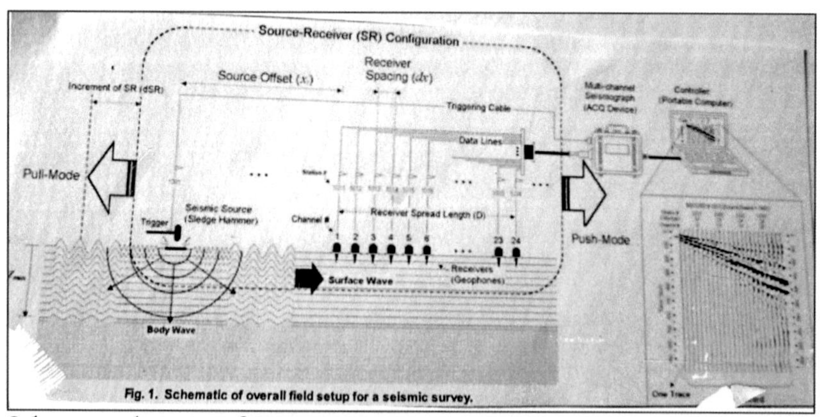

Fig. 1. Schematic of overall field setup for a seismic survey.

Schematic diagram of Seismic Survey

Source: Wikipedia

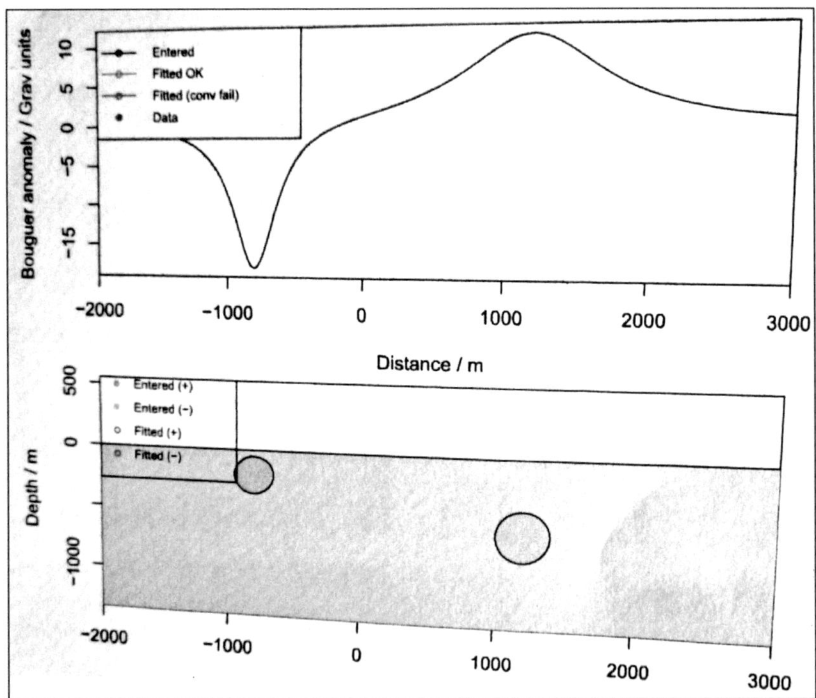

Schematic diagram of Gravity Survey

Source: Wikipedia

The differences in the force of gravity are measured by a *relative* gravity meter. After correction for differences in altitude and latitude the density of the rock below the meter is plotted by the geophysicist'

The line of the gravity survey is measured and mapped by the surveyor. The surveyor also records latitude and the ground heights.

The gravity survey uses a smaller workforce and requires less equipment than the seismic survey and is accordingly is cheaper and quicker. However the seismic survey gives more information on the earth's structure and is a more reliable

Papuan Explorer discharging cargo off Kerema

A.P.C. boat *M.V.Darega* at Omati wharf on Omati River

S.S.Papuan Explorer at anchor off Kerema

indicator of where the underground *traps,*that might hold oil, exist.

Papua is a land of many rivers and many swamps and with its high rainfall working in the bush was difficult. There were no roads to use for deliveries of supplies and equipment. To supply and service their field operations, searching for oil Australasian Petroleum Company were heavily reliant upon river transport and had to establish what was virtually their own navy.

As the activities increased A.P.C. bought the *Hannis Ven (Papuan Explorer)* to extend their own supply line back to Australia. The *Papuan Explorer* discharged her cargo on to smaller ocean going ships, that needed reliable navigation charts of the rivers used to deliver to the field parties.

The people to lead the search were brought to Papua, on contract, mainly from the United Kingdom, Australia and the United States of America. Physical workers were recruited from the villages. The Papuans had proved reliable and effective as soldiers and carriers during World War 2 and were well able to support the professional teams.

The professionals were geophysicists, surveyors, medical aides, pilots, mechanics and native labour officers. They lived in field base camps located throughout the territory with their headquarters in Port Moresby the capital of Papua New Guinea.

Where useable the field parties had dugout canoes (shaped by ax and by adze from red cedar trees), Seine boats (small inboard motor boats used normally as fishing boats) and *bomb scows* (flat bottomed hulls that serviced the world war 2 flying boats with bombs, fuel and supplies) to carry and deliver equipment and supplies to the teams when out on survey. When water transport was not possible all provisions were carried overland by native labour.

Major supplies were brought to the base camps by ocean-going ships. Personnel and urgent freight were flown from Port Moresby by Catalina flying boats that were on lease from QANTAS. One field party (Seismic One) used contracted Bell helicopters to distribute equipment and dynamite to their survey lines.

Apart from the Headquarters and camp at Badili in Port Moresby A.P.C. had two seismic survey parties in the field (Seismic One at Aramia ,and Seismic Two at Totoma). There was one gravity party at Tarara on the Wassi Kussa, a deep drilling rig at Omati on the Omati River and a shipping facility at Napa Napa across the bay from Port Moresby.

One of the first post WW2 APC surveys was at Aitape in 1947. This original Seismic One survey party was an operation run by Darcy Exploration. They were surveying for the Anglo Iranian Oil Company which later became British Petroleum.

B.P. had begun searching for oil in Papua in 1948 having previously searched in Persia, now Iran. Two of the 1954 Seismic One members Phil Bliaux, Party Chief, and Harry Strudwick, in charge of native labour, had worked with the D'Arcy Exploration Seismic One team in 1948.

Papua posed a problem that had not existed in Persia. In Persia people employed as assistants and as labourers were generally educated and experienced. In Papua the only labour available was the young men living in the villages close to the exploration sites. These men had very little education and no experience as assistants or labourers on oil search.

The Challenge

What it was like to be a surveyor working on the search for oil in Papua it is useful to consider four relevant aspects. One is what did some men who had done these surveys report? Another was what was the field procedure? another is what were the hazards confronted and another, what were the fears and phobias experienced.

In 1976 S.E.Reilly reported that “Papua had the world’s largest swamps and that tropical heat and humidity made physical exertion unpleasant. He reported that surveying was hampered by heavy rainfall and exuberant vegetation and further that malevolent insects, reptiles and parasites were a menace to the surveyor’s health and comfort.”

In 1960 Charles Blakemore was in Papua as an oil exploration surveyor with British Petroleum. He described this period of his surveying career as a nightmare. He refers to a constant fear of either being killed by the locals or bitten by snakes and eaten by crocodiles. He reports that he was thrown in at the deep end with a team of natives with whom he could not communicate.

Peter Best was the survey boss when I was with Seismic One at Aramia on the Aramia River. He had worked for some years as a surveyor in the field before he became more occupied in the base camp organising the surveys for the geophysicists. Peter wrote what was more a description of what he thought was how the surveyors on oil search worked.

He wrote that the surveyors were generally young men who served for one fourteen month term. Their task was to survey 3,000 feet per day. He thought that surveyors spent most of their time waiting for the cutting of *dalas* to be completed. Sorties usually lasted a couple of weeks with an early morning start and with the team working until dark. A cook would be left in the camp to prepare an evening meal and dry biscuits were available during the day.

Based on his estimate of 3,000 feet of survey a day and a sortie of two weeks, the result would be only seven miles. This must be working in dense and difficult jungle. I did surveys through swamp and through timbered bush, both dense and light, and some sorties were fifty miles long. Cutting through bamboo would be the most difficult but I only encountered bamboo in clumps and never as a complete forest.

Comparing my experience with the procedure outlined by Peter Best I assume that he is referring to working in more difficult bush than what confronted my team. I rarely made early starts to a day and only on a few occasions did I survey until it was dark. When the bush was difficult we combined transfer of the camp and the cutting of the *dala*. In swamps and light timber the cutting and the survey always moved at the same pace without stops or pauses.

Field Procedure

Seismic surveying for the surveyor was straight line surveying through bushland. This meant that regardless of the sort of country you were working in it was necessary to clear a *dala* that gave a straight line of sight station to station.

In grass swamps where the grass was usually head high two boys working side by side bend the grass forward. The following boys with bush knives would cut the grass off at water level. Generally the theodolite‘s tripod would be long enough to have the instrument above water level. On occasions, in deep water, it was necessary to mount the instrument on a tree stump. The continuing problem in swamp surveying was the loss of level when any traffic came close to the theodolite. Tripod legs wrapped in grass and standing on soft ground reacted to any movement.

In sago swamps the water was usually only a few feet deep and presented no problem. The sago palms were not cut down as a line of sight could be achieved by trimming the fronds form the trunk. This was a slow process because the hands of hard sharp thorns along the frond had to be pressed into the ground to avoid contact with the barefooted survey line. On the two surveys on which I had sago swamps

I called a halt so that the boys cut down a sago palm and did the necessary pounding to collect the sago flour.

Tony Crawford who is an authority on the area between the Fly and the Aramia rivers where the Gogodalas live wrote in his book AIDA " Of all the vegetation within the Gogodals cosmos, it was the sago palm that provided the incentive for the Gogodala to cease wandering in search of a home. It was directly responsible for a later migration that dispersed the community, thus creating the evolvement of today's clans, and as always it has supplied the Gogodala's staple-sago flour.

Besides being the main source of food, the sago palm is invaluable as a provider of material for house-building, items of dress, and, as a totem, is a spiritual link with it. The massive arch roofs were solely of sago leaf thatch, and all the walls made of sago frond mid rib. Only the flooring and the poles were from another source.

Today the sago palm remains as equally important to their society as it was in former times, continuing to provide the main elements of existence, nourishment and shelter."

When I stopped work to allow a sago flour party I did not realise how important it was to my Gogodala team. This probably helped to make their leader, Anciani a better friend.

From the Bensbach River at the most western region of Papua to the Fly River the country is mainly swamp and savannah with some strips of large trees near the Fly River. North and east of the Fly River are some of the world's largest swamps. These extend to the Aramia River and this area is Gogodala homeland. North and east of the Aramia River there are some heavily timbered areas and some of these trees are too large to be cut down for a survey line of sight. I experienced this problem on only one occasion and cutting large vees into the three trees involved was the answer.

One heavily timbered area was surveyed after a period of heavy rain and the depth of water in the valley between two ridges required working out of a canoe. The *dala* was cut through the tree tops with bush knives.

Fears and Phobias

The fears and phobias referred to by Reilly and Blakewell reminded me of two men that I worked with in the field and who I now realise were not suited to working on their own on bush surveys. In Papua the nights were never without sounds of some kind and one distressed young man could not sleep if he could hear something. The other chap always wore a side arm which he kept under his pillow at night. Both of these men reacted in panic when faced with a minor emergency.

I had one problem with noises in the night and it was the tom tom of the boys when they had a music night with their drums. The answer to this was to make them camp well away from your own tent fly abode.

The Hazards

In Papua there are hazards and you had to be aware of them and behave to accommodate them. The most dangerous was the crocodile. They were rarely encountered and you almost always knew where they were and they could be avoided. Avoiding them when surveying through a swamp is not an option but I only saw one sign that a crocodile had crossed our path. On one island in a swamp we found a nest of six baby crocodiles, and no doubt the mother was somewhere nearby. It is believed that the mother crocodile keeps a constant watch over the eggs and probably this continues after hatching.

I encountered only one case of a crocodile taking a life and that was on the Kikori River where two village women were searching the banks for a child they said had been taken when swimming in the river.

Apart from the crocodiles there were plenty of predators that could be a problem. Some were insects like mosquitoes, mokka and sandflies and these were everywhere and protection was always needed. Less frequently met with were snakes, sharks and stingrays unless you were working on the coast where they were plentiful.

The most common problem was the leech that would be in the water or on the trees always ready to feed on your blood. Chemicals were available to prevent this but in the swamps they were almost unavoidable.

Hookworm could be avoided by not going about barefooted and close inspection of your bed and clothing before use was protection against scorpions.

Snakes usually move away when you approach them and leave them alone and don't stand on them and you are quite safe. Although I only saw a snake on one occasion it was a spectacular proof that there were lots of snakes and they could be anywhere.

One morning at the start of a survey near the Soari River we crossed a small grass swamp about fifty metres across. In crossing we trampled the grass down for about four metres width. On our return in the afternoon there at least fifty snakes of all types distributed over the path we had made in the morning. Apparently they were attracted to the opportunity to laze in the sun. My normally fearless Gogodala team would not go near them so it was left to their intrepid leader to scare the snakes away. We must have walked over a lot of snakes in the morning without knowing.

Reflecting upon the recollections of Reilly and Blakewell and taking into account the challenge of surveying in the Papuan bush with its hazards and the potential for fears and phobias I consider that we were fortunate to have had an almost trouble free year in the field.

We had three serious injuries, two of these were self inflicted accidents and the other was the shark attack while hunting.

My own difficulties with *mokka* and leeches were the result of my not knowing that the prevention was in the medical kit. Travelling and camping on my own I would certainly have had a lot of trouble. As part of a team who knew how to travel and live safely in the bush I was sheltered and my trust had been rewarded.

Garden hut and village women in dugout canoe on the Omati River

Chapter 2
Fly River Swamps

Becoming A Taubada

It was possible to do the earlier years of a Civil Engineering Degree at the University of Queensland part time. This was not an option for me in my final year that had to be done full-time. To finance this I decided to work in 1954 to build a bank.

One of my part-time jobs was with the hydrographic section of the Queensland Irrigation and Water Supply Department. This probably influenced the A.P.C. decision to transfer me later from field survey with Seismic One to river survey on the M.V. Tiveri with Captain Baker.

In addition to the part-time work during the academic year I would go to Mount Isa Mines in Mount Isa for the required ten week vacation work experience. This, with the *lead bonus,* that was six times the weekly wage, when combined with my part time wage gave me a full and comfortable life style. That was about to change.

I had read an interesting article written by Colin Simpson, for the magazine A.M., about the A.P.C. seismic camp at Everill Junction on the Fly River. About the same time when A.P.C. had advertised requesting applicants for a position as an engineering assistant I decided that Papua New Guinea was an option for my 1954 year off.

I applied for the engineering assistant job but Vacuum Oil, who were partners with Australasian Petroleum Company and Oil Search, in the search for oil in Papua. Vacuum Oil decided that I did not have enough experience for the engineering assistant job. However they offered me a position as an unlicensed surveyor in Papua which I accepted.

Accordingly I flew out of Brisbane at 11.30 pm on the first of May 1954 in a QANTAS Skymaster. We landed at Port Moresby at six thirty am on the following day.

The reception at Jackson Field was dramatic. There was a large crowd assembled with the Police Band and ranks of police constables lined up to welcome us. I was much impressed but the 'us' turned out to be Cardinal Gilroy and his party who left the left the plane while we waited on board as requested.

Port Moresby turned out to be pretty much what I had expected. Two hotels and several well-appointed shops fronting concrete footpaths and sealed streets. Some of the local families could be seen either strolling around or lounging on the footpaths near the shops.

Papuan family, downtown Port Moresby

Family outside Koki markets, Port Moresby

Papuan policeman at Koki markets, Port Moresby

After arrival we went to the A.P.C. camp travelling along Ela Beach road past the Koki market to Badili about three miles from Port Moresby.

The scene at Koki and the Koki market was very different to what I saw in the town centre of Port Moresby.

Koki Village and Koki markets were on the road to Badili at the end of the Ela Beach road. Built in the bay the village houses were 'built on stilts. This was to have the convenience of living over the water and coping with the

Children at Koki markets, Port Moresby

Mother and daughter outside Koki markets, Port Moresby

Koki markets, Port Moresby

Girl and fishing boat in Koki Bay, Port Moresby

rising tides. On market days the Koki market was packed with customers and their families plus the villager vendors. Probably thirty odd fishing *lakatois* moored in the water adjacent to the covered market place. Fresh vegetables, fish, lobsters and probably betel nut were all available.

Everybody, including the policeman, was barefooted. The men were wearing *ramis* (a one piece loin cloth). Most of the women were topless. It was a family day with children of all ages enjoying the occasion.

Further along the Hubert Murray highway and less than three miles from Port Moresby was Badili where the South Pacific Brewery was located on Scratchley Road. Across the road from the brewery was the Australian Petroleum Company's offices and camp facility. The camp had been a wartime barracks and mess. A short distance further along the road was the village of Kila where the original Port Moresby aerodrome had been located.

During World War 2 this strip was upgraded and was known as the Three Mile. It was used by the Third Bomb Group when they flew in from Charters Towers in Queensland to go on bombing missions against the Japanese.

Having arrived at Badili I was introduced to my 'personal boy' and issued with a field box and several items that were for use in the field on survey. The personal boy was named Dagleesi he came from Rabaul and for the short time I was in Badilli he went well.

After three days in Badili I flew out of Port Moresby on a QANTAS Airways Catalina bound for Totoma on the Fly

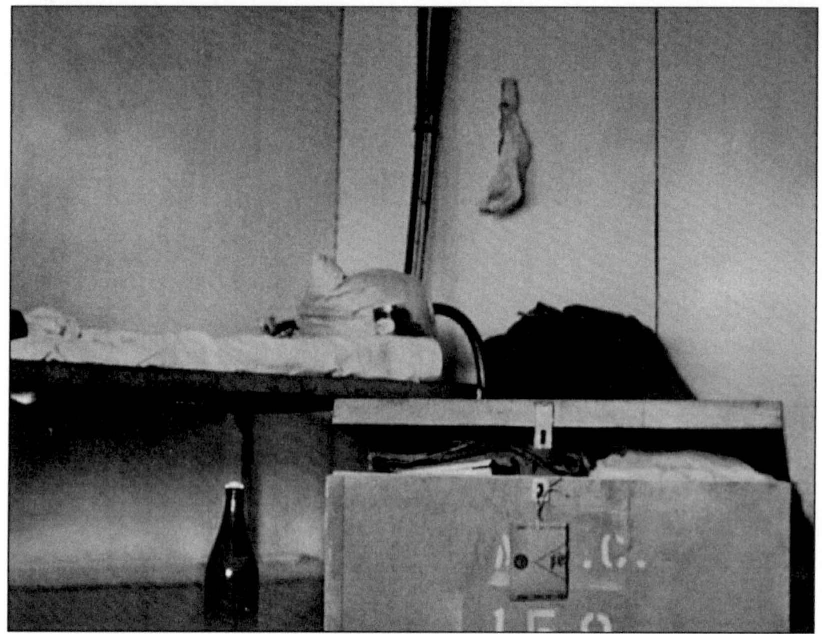

Field box and bed, A.P.C. base camp Badili, Port Moresby

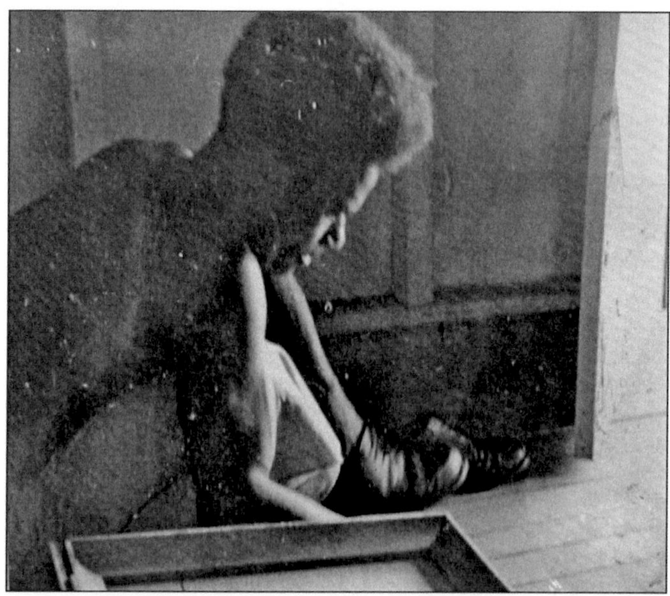

Personal boy Dagleesi from Rabaul at Badili, Port Moresby

Harry Strudwick at Everill Junction, Fly River. Seismic One.

Catalina flying boat VH EBC *Island Chieftain* at Port Moresby

Survey team on a *Bomb Scow* at Totoma on the Fly River

Suki village survey team at island camp in the Fly River swamp

Canoe in *dala* from Red Bank to the Fly River swamp survey line

Author's first camp on the Fly River swamp survey View A

Author's first camp on the Fly River swamp survey View B

River. I had been allocated to Seismic Two who were based at Totoma. The Catalina VH-EBC *Island Chieftain* flew via Middleton and Kikori before alighting on the Fly River at Everill Junction where its tributary, the Strickland River, joins it.

The weather had deteriorated on the flight from Port Moresby and after a short visit to the Seismic One Base camp at Everill Junction we flew back to Port Moresby. Two days later we flew direct to Burei Creek on the Fly River and a seine boat delivered us to the Seismic Two base camp at Totoma.

First Survey

At Totoma I was introduced to Imigi who came from Lake Suki about sixty miles up the Fly River from Totoma. Imigi was my personal boy for all my time with Seismic Two. While he did not have the domestic skills of Dagleesi he was friendly and anxious to please. His skill on the water with a dugout canoe later gave me one of my most memorable and pleasant experiences in Papua.

On the 12th of May Bill Love a trainee surveyor and I travelled by seine boat to Redbank. Redbank was a field camp about twenty five miles upstream from Totoma. The access *dala* through the swamp to the survey line started nearby and dynamite for the seismic survey was stored temporarily at Redbank.

Our first survey camp was at the intersection of the access *dala* and the survey line. It was in the swamp and a platform for my bed and storage of all provisions was built from long, spindly paper bark trees. Overnight the structure would settle into the swamp. This required the cross timbers to be raised and re-tied to keep the bed and provisions out of the water. The bed was a tube of canvas supported by two horizontal poles that were tied to poles sunk into the swamp.

The provisions consisted of bags of flour, dried peas (beanies),rice and salt plus boxed tinned beef. Sufficient of these items were carried to feed the survey line for the expected time on the survey. In this case all these goods plus tent flies, cooking and medical items were carried into the survey line in dugout canoes.

The surveyor chose food to his own liking from what was available in tins at the base camp store. These items plus a bed roll and a tin box for personal items and cigarettes were sorted into 40 pound loads for the carriers.

Surveying in the marsh presented problems with the ability to set up the theodolite. Water depth sometimes made use of the tripod impossible and the use of a tree as a base or a support then became necessary.

Bill Love had been forced to abandon work on this survey line when his labour team lost interest in continuing with the survey. This was a reaction to the realisation that the swamp had not ended as they had assumed it had. When they came to what proved to be an island after days of problems in deep swamp the *boys* built a comfortable camp and were happy for the time being. However two days later they were back into the swamp and Bill decided to return to Totoma after only a few more days of survey.

As noted earlier surveying in the Papuan bush is a challenge and working in swamps is one of problems that had to be overcome. If the workers do not want to work in the swamps then it is not possible to do the survey. It is important to consider who the workers are and what is needed to build a loyal team of workers prepared to accept such difficulties.

The Workers

The workers are the Papuan native villagers who make up the teams on seismic or gravity surveys. They carry the loads from camp to camp and do any necessary clearing of the survey line with axe or bush knife.

They are indentured for eighteen months and at the end of that time they are returned to their village. While employed they are accommodated and fed are paid a set sum of cash.

They are recruited by the company supervisors from the villages near the field base camp. They are the young and are the fittest men and boys available and when in a survey team they are referred to as a *boyline* regardless of their age.

In addition to carrying the diminishing quantity of daily food supplies the team carries some loads for the whole trip. Tent flies, Wireless, batteries, theodolite, bedding, lamps, field box, medical kit, and drums of fuel constitute many forty pound *boy-loads.*

When comparing the standard of workers available in Papua with those available in Persia James Sinclair in his book *Masta Mak* quoted the Anglo Iranian surveyors who saw advantage in being able to recruit educated and experienced survey teams. The surveyors in Papua were better off with the inexperienced and untrained Papuan villager. The Papuan villagers were comfortable with the climate and the environment and they often supplemented their rations by hunting wild life in their bushland. Also they were more than capable of doing the work.

Care, Food and Accommodation

The success of a survey depends upon the willingness and the ability of the team to do he work. For us the work was carrying, cutting and setting up camps. Sometimes this had to be done under difficult circumstances so the team had to be fit and healthy.

Keeping the team fit and healthy was the surveyor's responsibility and that necessarily meant providing care and nourishment. Care involved attending to any injuries, avoiding small scratches and bites turning into ulcers, adequate rest, some recreation and supplying the full food rations.

The ability to look after injuries was limited to cleaning up, applying *brilliant green*, and bandaging wounds when required. One medical call was the requirement that each boy had cod liver oil every week. Most of the team did not like the taste of the cod liver oil so I always made this a formal parade, only moving to the next in line after the tablespoon of oil had been swallowed.

Once the food was issued I left how and when it was eaten to the team. I never issued food rations for too many days ahead because it was likely it would all be eaten immediately and we would run out of food before we finished the survey. I did on one occasion when we had more loads than boys break this rule. The extra food distributed among the team brought the loads and boys equation into balance.

We never stopped for a midday meal and I ate a small tin of sardines each day about midday or earlier if I was hungry. On a few occasions all work stopped so that we could hunt something that had been sighted for fresh food.

In suitable country there would be a couple of *out-riders* away from the line looking for a pig, cus-cus, cassowary or goura pigeon and one would have the shot gun just in case. The goura pigeon is said to be the world's largest pigeon. It has a large lace like top knot and it is attractive as well as being a delicacy.

When surveying close to the Aramia River we had plenty of crocodile meat and unknown to me at the time the boys were enjoying crayfish while my personal boy was serving me hot tinned Irish stew.

Bill Love when he had to go back into the swamp after setting up camp on an island did not know was that he was surveying in what is known as the Fly-Diagoel Depression. This geological feature extends from the north bank of the Fly River north until the highlands. It is a vast swamp with occasional high ridges. Between the Fly and the Aramia Rivers these high ridges where the Gogodalas planted coconuts and established their villages.

Bill who spoke Motu and had native labour experience was with me to initiate me in the role of a seismic surveyor in the Papuan bush. Together we resumed his earlier survey and after a few days in the swamp we came to another island.

Here we enjoyed dry comfort and hot cooked meals. Unfortunately this ended when Bill shot himself in the foot with his 22 rifle when stalking something that had kept him awake with its repetitive call. Earlier in the night he had woken me up to blast the base of a small shrub where he thought the sound was coming from. Two blasts from our hunting shot gun trimmed the shrub , swept the ground and ended the sound. Unfortunately that was not the end of the problem, because I was later woken up by the sound of a shot and Bill's shout that he had been shot. I have later learned that Bill had been annoyed by the croak of a frog.

He had smashed the little toe on his left foot and he attempted to ignore the problem. Unfortunately foot swelled and became painful so we agreed that he should go back to Totoma. He took a canoe and a few boys and he wished me good luck as he set off.

I really must have enjoyed good luck because I was able to finish the survey on my own without any serious trouble. The language difficulty was eventually overcome by using the police motu dictionary that I kept under my hat. This sufficed because the team knew what they had to do and went about their work without any need for instructions from me.

The straight survey line was maintained by taking a sighting on to the previous station or marker and projecting this line forward by plunging (rotating the telescope on its horizontal axle so that the eyepiece was now pointing back towards the previous station. The *planky* (the boy with the staff),who was forward with the cutters advancing the *dala,* could be lined up with the telescope's vertical cross-wire so as to maintain the straight line. At appropriate distances the team would assemble lengths of timber to mark either a geophone station or a shot point as required.

The *dala* was progressed by three boys each with a stick held horizontal falling forward to bend the grass. Once the grass was pushed over the rest of the team would cut the grass above water level.

On one occasion we crossed what was a smaller cross *dala* in the grass at right angles to the survey line. When this happened it was not good news to learn, after going to my book, that *huala* was crocodile.

Two unwise decisions I made about what to wear made the task more difficult. The first mistake was to wear U.S. Army lace up gaiters. Not only did they let the leeches onto my legs but they meant that each trouser leg became full of water. This was an extra load to carry and the increased size of the inflated leg increased the effort required when walking in the swamp.

The other mistake was to think that if it was a good thing for athletes to wear an 'athletic support' then it would be a good thing for a surveyor on long treks to also wear an athletic support. Unfortunately the tight fitting waist and leg straps were ideal areas for the scrub *mokka* to make a home under the skin. This resulted in an itchy rash of little pink mounds that defined the strap locations.

After three weeks, when I returned to Totoma I learnt that included in the medical kit was a bottle of di-butyl

Sick Australian soldier and medical aide, New Guinea WWII

thallial. Had I applied this liquid to my body I would have had no trouble with the *mokka* or the leeches.

Fortunately for me the *mokka* that had invaded me were not carrying the scrub typhus virus that some *mokka* carried. The scrub typhus was generally fatal and it had a problem during the New Guinea campaign in WWII. The di-butyl thallial was developed as the answer to this problem.

Wearing the gaiters and not having access to any leeches sucking blood meant that the leech would be free to fill

Left hander Max Chisholm helps cut *dala* through bamboo

up with blood undisturbed before it dropped off. Each day when I stripped to dry out and change there would be as many as seven leeches in my socks.

Only on one occasion while surveying was I aware of any blood flowing from my body and when this happened I was shocked and worried. We had come to an island and as I emerged from the swamp I saw that the front of my trousers over a large area was covered in blood. I diagnosed this as a stone in the kidney which would have been a problem so far from help. I undressed to discover that the blood was

Author with side arm (rigged for left hander) and Suki cook boy Imigi

Author at end of the Fly River swamp survey. Shot point 707

Max Chisholm with Goura pigeon

flowing from my penis and to my relief one of my Suki men said *domo taubada.* A leech was a lot less trouble than a stone in the kidney so these were the most welcome words I heard while in Papua.

A leech drops off after it has filled with blood and depending upon the leech and where it attacks you determines how long you bleed after the leech drops away. This could vary from fifteen minutes to two hours. Judging by the amount of blood on my clothes I had been bleeding for longer than the fifteen minutes.

A leech that gets as far as the bladder can cause death. A leech leaves a slit where his non sucking end anchors itself while sucking blood. In my case the anchor slit in the skin could be seen outside so I had no reason to worry about that. The Sukis, who were lake and swamp dwellers, told me that leeches entering the bladder has been a problem with them. For women it was more likely. For that reason they always wore a palm leaf barrier when in the water.

Shortly after this incident we reached the end of the survey line, shot point 707, which we marked and then lost no time in getting back to the access *dala* and Redbank.

Although there had been a lot of evidence that there were crocodiles in the area we never sighted any of them in the swamp. We did however, near shot point 707, come across a nest with lots of baby crocodiles. I got one as a souvenir and the boys ate the others. Apparently the mother crocodile stays close to the nest to guard the eggs so it is wise to stay well clear of a crocodile nest.

Redbank to Totoma by Canoe

Max Chisholm a native labour man who had brought the dynamite to Redbank joined me on the last day of the survey and returned to Redbank with me.

Apart from needing help to end my itching problem I was looking forward to a cold beer and late in the afternoon I decided to paddle back to the base camp with Imigi my personal boy. Max decided to join us and so the four of us paddled out to the middle of the Fly River and headed south.

Probably because he saw how little free board we had Max dropped his paddle and started yelling and crying out in panic. He wanted to go straight back to the bank but like Redbank the near bank was about fifteen feet high and landing there was impossible. All four of us would have drowned attempting to put him ashore immediately.

I gave Max a pretty rude message and advised him to shut up and wait until we rounded the next bend. When we were able to beach the canoe we said goodbye to him without any concern about how he would get back through the bush to where we had started from.

It was now dark and I checked with Imigi if he was happy to continue because this was a complete role reversal. From now on I would do what Imigi thought was the thing to do. Imigi was happy to continue so we paddled back midstream and set off. We now had a little bit more freeboard and with only an occasional stroke with the paddles we were making many knots.

Imigi being a Suki was a river boy from birth and I was happy to trust his ability to keep us upright and without overtaking and colliding with a floating log. In the Fly River trees were often seen being swept downstream after having slipping into the river as part of an eroding bank .

I believed that he would know when we passed Burei Creek that joined the Fly River a short distance north of Totoma. I trusted him to have us on the right side of D'Albertis Island to get to Totoma.

This canoe trip from Redbank to Totoma, despite the bad start, was my most enjoyed experience during my year in Papua. The small bushes along the river's edge were covered with fireflies and as we sped along the bushes seemed to be rotating.

Imigi definitely realised that he was running the show and he displayed this by teaching me two songs to keep me happy. One in motu *Hanua Kikeni* (The Village Girls). The other was more a chant from the Suki song book. It went 'Doogie Roma, Doogie Roma, Doogie, Doogie, Doogie, Row-ah-mar. He never told me what I was singing about, probably a popular head hunting song.

There was still one Coleman lamp burning in the camp when we drifted into the Totoma jetty. Imigi took off to my 'donga' to light my Coleman lamp and rig my bed and mosquito net before joining his mates where no doubt he had some good tales to tell.

After showing my spotty body and listening to the joyful appraisal I was given I got the sad news that Seismic Two had been out of beer for two weeks. The last half inch in a bottle of gin was all I got. Part of the appraisal was to learn about mokka and I realised I had seen them every time I read the theodolite vernier through magnification. The little scarlet demons were always scurrying between to the top and bottom plates of the instrument.

The *mokka* a tiny scarlet coloured crab-like insect was sometimes a carrier of scrub typhus that, when not treated early was a killer disease. Di butyl thallial applied to the skin protected you against *makka.* It will also stop leeches attaching themselves to your body.

One of the accepted methods of getting a leech off your body is to apply heat with a match or cigarette to the leech. Expert opinion is that to do that you could cause a possibly disease carrying leech to discharge its body contents into the wound and that would initiate a serious infection. The recommended method of leech removal is to scrape it off with a finger nail or a knife. How long you bleed after a leech drops off depends upon how much anti-coagulant remains and from where the blood was taken.

Seismic Two was a small party of eight and generally things were relaxed and evening meals were always friendly and pleasant occasions. One evening shortly after my return from the swamp survey this atmosphere was lost. We were joined that evening by a visiting native labour officer named John Senior. True to form Senior started to bait and bully the medical aide, a quiet friendly chap who I remember as spending most of his spare time practising his golf swing.

The other surveyor at the table was Noel Elliot a tall gangling laconic man from Gippsland in Victoria, Elliot told Senior to shut up as we had all had enough of him. No one was supposed to talk to Senior like that so he told Elliot he had better come outside and say that. Probably to Senior's surprise Elliot got up and went outside. Senior followed him and we all stayed at the mess table. After a lot of cursing and the sound of fists and boots hitting bodies much to everybody's surprise it was Noel Elliot who returned to the table and finished his meal.

Senior who had come to Totoma with a load of dynamite did not come to breakfast, having left in his *bomb scow* at first light. He had a reputation for getting enjoyment out of terrorising people, bolstered no doubt by the presence of his big Alsatian dog.

It was no surprise to learn later that he had a close shave at Omati when a large drill tool that had fallen (?) from the top of the drill rig missed him by only a few feet. If some of the stories told about him were true it is amazing that he was able to retire in good health and run a shop and trade store at Kikori.

The Second Survey

I was transferred to Seismic One on the Aramia River with one survey link to make before going to Aramia by the landing barge GUBA.

The link was for a survey line that crossed the Isura River which entered the Fly River not many miles south of Totoma. The Seismic Two party chief assured me that the Seine boat boy knew the spot and that he would take me next morning.

Travelling to what I thought was Isara Dubaracue was a pleasant boat trip in a green wonderland. In mid-afternoon I asked how much further we had to go. The boat boy told me that he did not know and he had assumed that I had known. As I had no provisions and no bedding with me I returned to Totoma. Nobody ever enquired about the survey so I let it go and packed my gear for the transfer to Seismic One

Landing barge *Guba, Bomb scow and Seine boat* at Totoma jetty

Chapter 3
North of the Fly River Seismic One at Aramia

Totoma to Aramia

A week after completing the swamp survey and the Isara River excursion I was on board the ex-army landing barge GUBA off Kiwai Island travelling to Seismic One located on the Aramia River.

On the first night out of Totoma we tied up at Madiri, a former missionary station plantation, managed for over twenty years by Mr and Mrs Freshwater after it was gifted to the Unevangelised Field Mission by the Papuan Independent Limited in 1902. Situated on the south bank of the Fly River opposite Gaima on the north bank it was the first U.F.M. station in New Guinea. Madiri was the U.F.M.'s headquarters and the base for their penetration into the area between the Fly and the Aramia Rivers.

Tom Holland, a crocodile shooter, was now the part owner of Madiri where he ran a trade store along with his cattle farm and rubber plantation. We dined with Tom and his Papuan wife and later that night, after admiring his about forty different hand-guns, we went on a crocodile shoot along the Kiwai Island shoreline.

The search involved travelling slowly inshore in a small inboard boat and sweeping the water's edge with a spotlight. When the light shone on a crocodile its eyes glowed red and the kill began. Tom with a 303 rifle and his assistant were side by side up in the prow of the boat as it quietly approached the crocodile. When only a few feet from the reptile Tom pulled the trigger.

The assistant held a harpoon with a barbed steel head that came away from the harpoon after the *boy* speared the crocodile. This was done simultaneously with the sound of the shot. The barbed head was attached to the boat by a wire rope and so it was possible to retrieve the prize who would normally sink and be lost if not on this leash.

The smaller crocodiles are hauled on board after their jaws are taped together. The larger ones are collected by a bigger boat and taken ashore for skinning. The skin is removed from the carcass by cutting along the back and along the underside of the legs. With the big crocodiles the horny middle section of the back is too difficult to remove. This is left by making two parallel cuts either side of what is the animal,s armour.

The Seismic One base camp was upstream on the Aramia River so GUBA had to go into the Gulf of Papua to enter the

Aramia via the Bamu River. Crossing the gulf in a landing barge was a rough and windy adventure, so much so that The captain of GUBA lost his four laying hens when their coop on top of his cabin was blown overboard.

On the second night out GUBA tied up at the Unevangelised Field Mission located at the junction of the Bamu and the Aramia Rivers. We were shown over the 'long house' and entertained to dinner by Mrs Hardy, the missioner's wife and a visiting wife from another mission station. The food was excellent but our enjoyment was somewhat diminished by realising that we were under the keen scrutiny of our hosts. This was because the serving girls were very young and very topless. Normally we were accustomed to this, but at table the regular arrival and the proximity of a bosom over one's left shoulder was a serious distraction.

Aramia The Organisation — The People

It was never a surprise to arrive at the Seismic One base because well before reaching Aramia a flotilla of beer bottles would be met. Seismic One was a big party with some good drinkers with lots of 'dead marines' from the previous night and the boys had fun throwing them into the river below the mess.

Seismic One was a bigger and better equipped operation than Seismic Two. They had helicopters, more Seine boats,

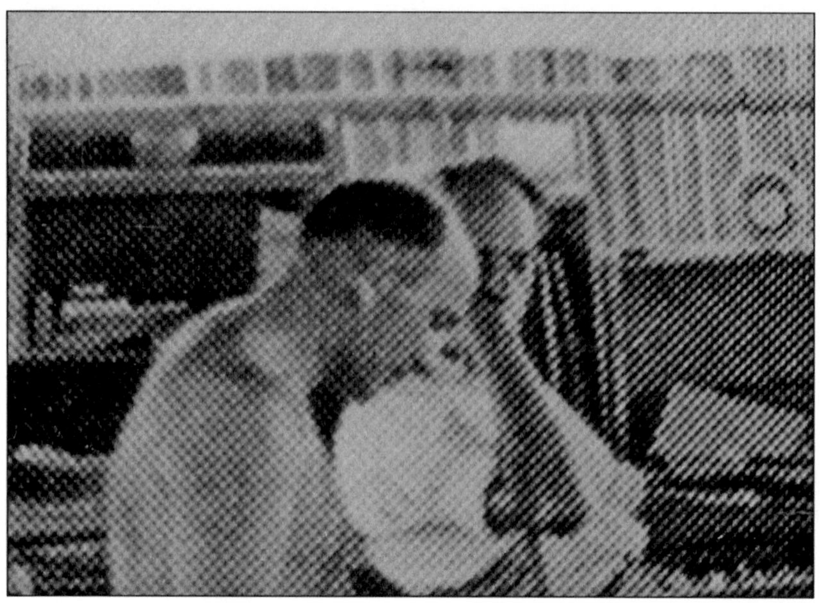

Major Leslie Philip Bliaux, BSc, M.B.E., M.M
British Petroleum, Melbourne

more bomb scows and a large number of dugout canoes equipped with 25 horse power Johnson outboard motors.

The team comprised seismic scientists, surveyors, mechanics, pilots, medical aides and native labour specialists leading carrier lines and heliport builders.

The party chief was Phil Bliaux a Cambridge University science graduate who had a distinguished WWII army career as Major Bliaux DSO, on special operations in the British Royal Corps of Signals. He served in India, Egypt and Greece and on two occasions he had been parachuted behind the German lines to help the Greek resistance fighters.

In Europe after D day he led his battalion into the Arnhem battle that went into history as the story in *Bridge*

Too Far the book by Cornelius Ryan. Phil's battalion was part of the 1st British Division that had suffered 7,872 casualties from 10,005 men at Arnhem. He knew too well the results of a bad plan and no doubt he would have always carried in his mind what his commander Lt. General Frederick 'Boy' Browning had told General Bernard Montgomery "I think we may be going a bridge too far" when the battle plan for the 1st British Division was finalised.

At Aramia Bliaux's experience and ability was reflected in the way that the routine and the facilities came together to produce a well informed and effective operation. It was obvious that Seismic One was seriously looking for oil.

Volley ball every afternoon followed by a warm shower, small *kai* (finger food) and a cold beer preceded a three course dinner with friendly and interesting workmates.

A cockney man named Eddie Otterside ("This side not the other side") was always in good spirits and on one occasion this got him into trouble. During a medical schedule to Badili, Eddie cut into a call "Seismic Two to medical officer Badili, we have a case of syphilis, please advise." with "Seismic One to Seismic Two, send it up to us. We drink anything." Phil was not amused and Eddie quickly found this out. It wasn't the content of Eddie's message that concerned Phil but the breach of protocol. Royal Signallers could never allow such conduct.

Our helicopters were on contract from an Hawaiian company and the pilots were all from the United States. One of these, Fred, who had served in Korea on the evacuation of wounded was always on for a joke and a story. This probably caused the crash he had at one of the field heliports.

On that occasion unknown to the native labour man waiting to take delivery of some cargo, a can of orange juice became wedged under one of the helicopter's pedals. With all hands and feet committed Fred was unable to help himself and had only one pontoon on the landing platform. He needed someone to reach into the cabin to remove the can and was using head signals and lip reading messages trying to achieve this. Knowing Fred the native labour officer thought it was a great joke. Fred realised no one understood him and so he was not going to get anyone to help. He switched everything off and the helicopter toppled off the platform and the air was filled with bits of rotor and airframe. The carriers scattered and it took some time to get them back out of the bush. The helicopter required a complete rebuild.

Helicopters were useful in finding and catching Birds of Paradise that apparently frolicked around on the vine-covered tree tops. In the year I was in Papua I only saw two Birds of Paradise, one at distance flying with its plumes stretched out behind it and the other that I got from one of the boys in exchange for a shirt.

The Bell 47D-1 helicopters were all fitted with pontoons for water work and their emergency landing practices were spectacular. They practised engine failure by auto-rotating into a lake beside the base camp. Dropping from a good height they would sink behind a wall of water with only the rotors in sight before popping up like a cork.

Once a clearing had been made in the bush beside a shot point and a platform of logs built above tree stump height helicopters delivered the large quantities of dynamite quickly and safely. The alternative was repacking the dynamite into carrier- sized loads and moving it on foot or by canoe many miles from store to the shot point.

Field Incidents

The man in charge of all native labour at Seismic One was Harry Strudwick who had been featured in the Colin Simpson magazine article that had played a part in my decision to apply for a job in New Guinea.

Harry generally known as 'Struddy' was a small quietly spoken blond-headed man in his mid-forties who was universally respected, by his workmates but also by the hundreds of men and boys in his native labour force.

Advice he gave me one night over a beer in the Aramia mess helped me escape from a dangerous situation that I had got myself into by an error of judgement. Harry had told me that if native labour confronted me in anger it was important that I did not show fear.

Emboldened by what was really only a small amount of experience I started to micro-manage my carriers and *dala* cutters. One of the *boys* who was in fact old enough to be called a man rarely did more than make an occasional flick with his bush knife. I chastised him for not working and gave him a clip to the back of his head for good measure. Naturally he took offence at this and after throwing down his knife he picked up a big stick and with much shouting and yelling advanced on me.

Remembering Harry's advice I smiled and gambled by bending down in front of him and picked up his knife which I offered to him handle first.

I told him to stop shouting and to go back to work, to my relief and surprise he did. That was the only time that I raised my hand and in fact I never gave it a thought again.

Apparently when he was shouting angrily he was trying to get his mates involved but without success. That evening when he came to my tent with half a dozen cooked crayfish I realised that like me he was getting some good advice. He never became a big producer but he improved a bit and I never erred in that direction again.

I did however make one other mistake with the carrier line when I decided that one of the boys was not doing his share of the carrying work. I made sure that each load was the correct weight and that we had the right number of carriers. I did not realise that the team had the right to decide that one or more of their number did not have to carry. I would ensure that every one had a load only to discover at the end of the day that one of the team had carried two loads. Every time I acted the result was always the same so I realised it was better to forget it. I later learnt that there were many reasons why some of the team were always on 'light duties'.

It was no surprise that after returning to base camp Harry told me he had been given the full story of my incident during the survey. Without any comment or advice he let me know in his quiet calm way that he had the report.

My personal boy at Aramia was Aowa who was a good housekeeper and I always had clean clothes, a warm shower, a full Coleman lamp and when in the field a reasonable meal.

Aowa was not a Gogodala boy and apparently did not get along very well with the Gogodala team that I had. This plus an experience I had when with Seismic Two brought me close to shooting him one night near the Soari River.

The Seismic Two incident resulted from my tent fly being set up on a track leading to the river. Predictably a big light-coloured pig came into my tent one night and started to investigate the bags of flour and dried peas. It woke me up but as the shotgun was with the hunter in our team all I could do was to tell him to buzz (?) off and to make "go away" noises. He finally sauntered off and I decided that in future I would have the shotgun within reach for night intruders.

To escape the nightly drum concerts I always had the boys camp a long way from my camp. One night I woke up to see what I thought was a big light coloured pig under Aowo's kitchen fly close to my tent. This time I was armed and ready as I slowly advanced on my *pig*. Fortunately my mother had once told me about the danger of only wounding a wild pig as a result of her experiences growing up in the Queensland bush. The clue was to make sure it was a head shot and as I got really close I realised my *pig* was a badly rigged mosquito net moving with the wind. Aowo had sneaked back in the night and was asleep under the net in his kitchen.

The Aramia Survey and Crocodiles

After four days settling in at Aramia I was taken by Seine boat with a bomb scow carrying a fifteen boy line to Shot Point 15 on Samoki Creek. Shot Point 15 was the start point for the continuation of a partially completed survey line.

After crossing the Somaki Creek twice the depth of water on the line made progress impossible. The survey stopped for three days while a tree was cut down and a canoe shaped by trimming with an axe.

This pause in the trip allowed us to hunt and shoot three crocodiles before the completion of the dugout canoe allowed the survey to continue. It was at this stage working from a canoe in deep water, in what turned out to be a flooded valley, that we cut a *dala* that was in fact a tunnel through the tree tops.

Progress was slow until we were able to make a camp at Shot Point 18 and the Seine boat was released to return to Aramia down Somaki Creek. We then surveyed in heavily timbered country all the way to the Aramia River. We made camp (No.5) on the north side of the river when the Seine boat returned with supplies of flour, dried peas, rice and tinned meat.

Because the Gogodalas had eaten the three crocodiles we did not have any food shortage problems. Many villagers would only eat the tail meat of the crocodile but the Gogodala wasted nothing.

The Gogodalas come from a large group with many villages in the area of land and swamp between the Fly and the Aramia Rivers. This area is a flat flooded plain area with many river channels.

In his book AIDA Tony Crawford recounts the ground breaking voyage into this land by Sir Hubert Murray so that "we may appreciate the ugliness and the beauty of a small corner of the world on the world's greatest flood plain.

After his trip from the north bank of the Fly River to within a short distance of the Aramia River Murray wrote "I cannot imagine any people selecting such a place to live in." Crawford disagrees with Murray's assessment by stating "The flood plain of the Aramia has an abundance for all:

sago, fish, animal and bird life aplenty." Crawford could have included crocodile in his food list, for catching, cooking and eating all of the crocodile is one of the Gogodala man's special skills.

Anciani the leader of my labour team orchestrated his crocodile catching team with calm confidence that really was intrepid. When a crocodile sank to the bottom of a pond or river the procedure never varied. Anciani would locate the crocodile by searching with his feet in the area where the reptile had gone under. Having decided which way the reptile was facing Anciani would position eight or ten boys. They would stand forming an aisle along the path the crocodile would travel after Anciani gave it a prod with the much heavier stick he carried.

The disturbed crocodiles would swim just below the surface feet back and travelling fast to be met with sharp sticks from each side. The crocodile would leap out of the water with *boys* and sticks going in all directions. Anciani would run his three inch diameter spear down the crocs throat and the game was ended.

I saw this hand catching of crocodiles at least eight times and on two occasions on the shallow edge of a stream. There were no serious injuries but there were always bruises and abrasions from sticks or from a wildly swinging crocodile tail. In a river, depth would limit the number of sharp sticks that could be lined up as a reception aisle and the hunt would be called off.

These were food hunts and no attempt would be made to get a clean undamaged skin for the *taubada*. On shotgun

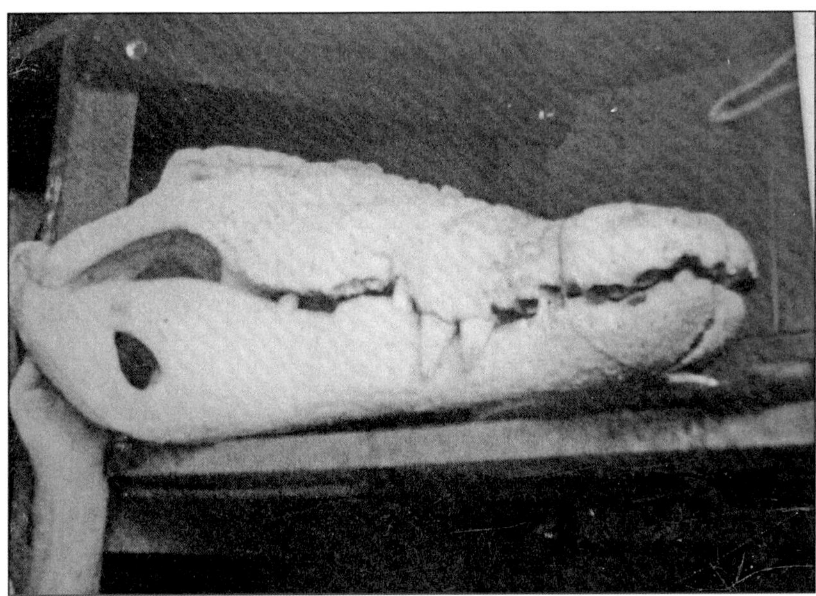

Crocodile Skull. Showing gap between jaws for bullet access to brain
R.S.Gilbert

Felling tree to make a dugout canoe

hunts the catch was shared with one complete skin for the *taubada* and one in turn for the team who wanted to leave the skin on the carcass This produced a pork-crackling like result after the crocodile was cooked .

We were on the upper Aramia River and apparently it had not been shot for a long time. That meant that as long as we travelled slowly and quietly in the Seine boat the crocodiles would stay on the bank. We would go hunting like this after a day's surveying and in four weeks I shot eight crocodiles.

The procedure was to select a crocodile of manageable size and without changing the beat of the motor run the boat prow into the muddy bank. It was important to avoid being directly in front of the crocodile for two reasons. One was if he got a fright he would go straight ahead and with the impact and the jaws anything could happen.

The other reason was to be positioned so that the *bird-shot* would get to the brain through the gap that a crocodile has in its skull just above where the upper and lower jaws meet. Ideally you would be slightly to one side, a few feet lower and about ten feet from its head. Bang, and the crocodile would flick over dead on the bank.

On one occasion after we had as usual ,put a crocodile at our feet in the boat it suddenly reared up and bit a foot long chunk of wood out of the gunwale. Quick action with an axe to its head restored order. From that day on we always taped the jaws to be sure.

The smashing of the crocodile's head after that incident showed why our procedure was so effective. When the skull was opened up the bird shot was seen to have penetrated the brain. In fact the cartridge fabric packing was also found.

I took part in a 'no gun' hunt with the boys on only one occasion. For me it was the most exciting experience of that year. For the boys I think they saw a new side to the *taubada.* It probably played a part in my escape from trouble when I made my mistake punishing the lazy *dala* cutter. This crocodile hunt started when the *boys* who had wandered away from the survey line looking for black palm ran back to the survey shouting for attention. They had found a nine to ten foot crocodile resting in a clear pool in the bush. The pool was only about thirty feet in diameter and only a few feet deep.

On this occasion it was decided that a chase was the best option so we all got our sharp sticks. Yes, me too. I was not going to miss this. The survey could wait. Anciani gave the crocodile his usual prod and the croc took off with fifteen boys and one surveyor in pursuit. It must have been terrified because it really did run away from us for probably twenty minutes. It had been bouncing off trees but kept running away. Eventually exhausted it turned and faced us with jaws wide open. Anciani ran his lance all the way down its throat. I led the cheering. I was a kid again and will always remember the joy we shared and the fun of being one of the *boys.*

The survey ended at geophone station 101, overcoming many problems, after the start at shot point 15. We had gone further than expected and in less time than planned. That meant there were some provisions that had not been consumed and these were stored at the geophone station 89 camp site on the bank of the Aramia River.

Some doubts had been expressed about our crocodile shooting successes but the quantity of fresh meat taken back to Aramia in the Seine boat ended these.

John Gordon who was responsible for making the helicopter clearings and platforms had to go upstream to GS 89 to collect the stored bags and boxes of food. He resented having to do this and that was the start of a personal problem that developed between John Gordon and me.

Soari River Survey

After a week in base camp finalising the field book, resting ,playing volley ball, enjoying small *kai,* and cold beer I was given another survey to complete.

I was taken by helicopter to a geophone station on survey line 39. Finding and doing a tie in survey was the first task before setting off to extend line 39.

There were no problems with the bush except for some slowing down in a sago swamp we came to after two days.

The water was shallow but the long hard spikes that covered the palm fronds were a serious problem for the bare footed team. This meant that after cutting off the frond it had to be turned over and pressed into the mud. There were lots of sago palms in the way and so this slowed us down.

On the other hand I declared a sago making holiday and having selected a likely tree it was cut down and opened up for the making of some extra food.

It was a few days after this that I made the mistake of using some physical discipline that created a heated and threatening situation. I now realise that rather than telling me off the angry carrier was trying to get some supportive action from his mates. He failed in this and the fact that Anciani, their leader, and I had a friendly working relationship would have been decisive.

Contrary to general opinion I had found the Gogodalas, overall, were anxious to please and to enjoy their surveying life with all its ups and downs.

Apart from my crocodile playtimes I had spent more non-working time with them than I had spent with any other of the teams that I worked with. One occasion was when I visited their camp at night to play *pis pis*. For the native Papuans playing cards was illegal, especially gambling in a card game. It was a simple game and the number able to play was only governed by the fact that there are only fifty two cards in a deck. Every player was dealt a card face down and when everyone had a card the betting began. The currency was small pieces of the Plantation Twist tobacco. I was made welcome because, as the man with a box of trade twist tobacco, I was new money in the school.

At the end I donated my winnings plus two fresh sticks from my *cunning-kick* (concealed reserve supply in case of a losing run) to the players. I was generous because I was not a user of twist tobacco and because my winnings appeared to have been at quite a few previous games.

There was no raising of a bet just those who thought they had a chance would put an extra piece of tobacco down and the hands were then shown. Suit did not matter and equal numbers shared the pool. There was a lot of cheering especially when the taubada won.

We had one other evening meeting which I called after being woken up by a loud crashing noise in my tent. The noise was the collapse of a fairly large table loaded with a radio, books, personal items etc. The table was made from lengths of branches side by side supported on two larger branches that sat on four legs planted in the ground.

Because it had been built in a hurry and not being very well made It had collapsed. I shouted at the top of my voice *memero eboni oi mai hurraga hurraga* (all boys come here quickly). To avoid the nightly drum concerts I had made them camp a long way from my tent. They heard me and came quickly expecting that I was in some trouble. When they saw the problem they thought it was funny until I told them to make me a new and better table.

In an hour after they had collected new materials I had a really robust replacement that set the standard for the rest of our time together.

The only trouble we had on this survey was that we were without radio contact for two weeks. We made good progress and finished after thirty days well ahead of our planned completion date. The end point was geophone station 90 that was two days' survey past our twelfth camp. We were all tired and anxious to get back to base camp.

We had been joined by the team that were making clearings and platforms for the helicopters. Keith, their native labour supervisor, thought that it would be a good idea if we started to do some clearing for him.

This did not suit our capabilities and our fitness so we walked out to the river and headed down the Soari River in outboard-powered dugout canoes.

A fine day plenty of freeboard and lots of speed was just what we needed. Anciani walked into an edge swamp with the shot gun and we had a cassowary to take home. It was a good trip and we arrived at Aramia at 7 pm that night.

John Gordon who was Keith's boss was upset at my decision to return with the survey team to Aramia rather than staying to help with the tree felling.

I was given a pretty rude lecture and that night after we all had plenty to drink he gave me a solid slap across the face. I was sitting and he stood over me, I guess, hoping for me to react. He was too big for any thoughts like that so I gave him my best 'Harry Strudwick type' smile and picked up my beer. Ignored he turned and walked out of the mess.

After two weeks of rest and routine in the base camp Phil sent me out to line 39 to survey a gap in the plot between geophone stations 102 and 110. They had been roughly located by cable lengths and better locations were required for the analysis of geophone records.

Catalina flying boat VH EBC Island Chieftain at Kauwis on the Bamu River

With two canoes and sixteen boys we were back in Aramia after four days and I was ready for my already overdue field break in Port Moresby.

Harry Strudwick joined me at the breakfast table to tell me that my survey team had done a *runner* overnight. They had taken some of their issued work equipment such as axes and a couple of canoes. I knew nothing of their planned departure but sensed that 'Struddy' thought otherwise. No doubt now that I was one of the Gogodala team he expected that I should feel some guilt at being let down

I had been warned when I joined Seismic One that the Gogodals could be difficult to work with and Harry Strudwick at that time gave me some advice that I think saved me from a serious problem on one occasion. Overall as a survey party we got along pretty well. This could have

Pedestrians and Top Pub, downtown Port Moresby

B25 Mitchell bomber Baby Blitz at 3rd Bomb Group base, Charters Towers

been because of our mutual interest in hunting crocodile or by my stopping work for sago parties.

These things would have helped but probably the more likely influence was Anciani's friendship with me combined with his capable leadership.

There are two aspects of the Gogodala culture that sets them apart from their near neighbours the Kiwai Islanders and the Suki Lake clan.

The most remarkable fact is that some Gogodalas think that they are descended from the lost tribe of Israel. Some even wear *yamulkas* and prayer shawls. Tudor Paritt from the Florida International University supports this contention but has been unable to prove it.

I can understand why some people agree with this idea. When I first met the Gogodalas I recognised several men who had classic Jewish facial features. The shape of the nose and the short jaw whiskers made it easy to believe that there could be a connection to a lost tribe if appearances meant anything. One explanation given for this similarity of appearance is that some very early visitors to New Guinea from the Middle East may have fathered children whose descendants are seen today among the Gogodala clans.

The other distinguishing fact is reported by Tony Crawford in AIDA where he writes about his research into the culture and history of the Gogodala. Crawford draws attention to the fact that "unlike their neighbours to the north and to the south the Gogodala claim emphatically that they have never practiced cannibalism, but do admit to being head-hunters. Heads both male and female among the slain were severed from the body using a bamboo knife and retained after curing as trophies. The head was actually skinned, the skull being removed and the skin then cured by smoking, after which the skin was stuffed with grass and sewn with cane."

Two days before my twenty fourth birthday I went on field break with Noel Elliot. Noel was the man who had been challenged by John Senior and who had given the bully a well justified hiding. We went by T boat to Kauwis at the mouth of the Bamu River and flew to Port Moresby in the Catalina *Island Chieftain* via Morehead and Wassi Kussa.

This was my first take off in a Catalina from a river. The possibility of hitting a floating log and the restricted clear water area eliminated the both engine run downwind during system checks. The alternative was one engine at a time with the boat in tight turns on the water. With the Catalina the blister turret would go beneath the water and sitting at the turret was quite an experience.

Before leaving Aramia I had shared a bottle of beer with a pale-faced, blue eyed stranger and it was only after he finally spoke did I realise that I was with Noel Elliot now without his long flowing full-face beard and almost shoulder-length hair. He did not look like a bloke that could cut John Senior down to size but he had done just that at Totoma.

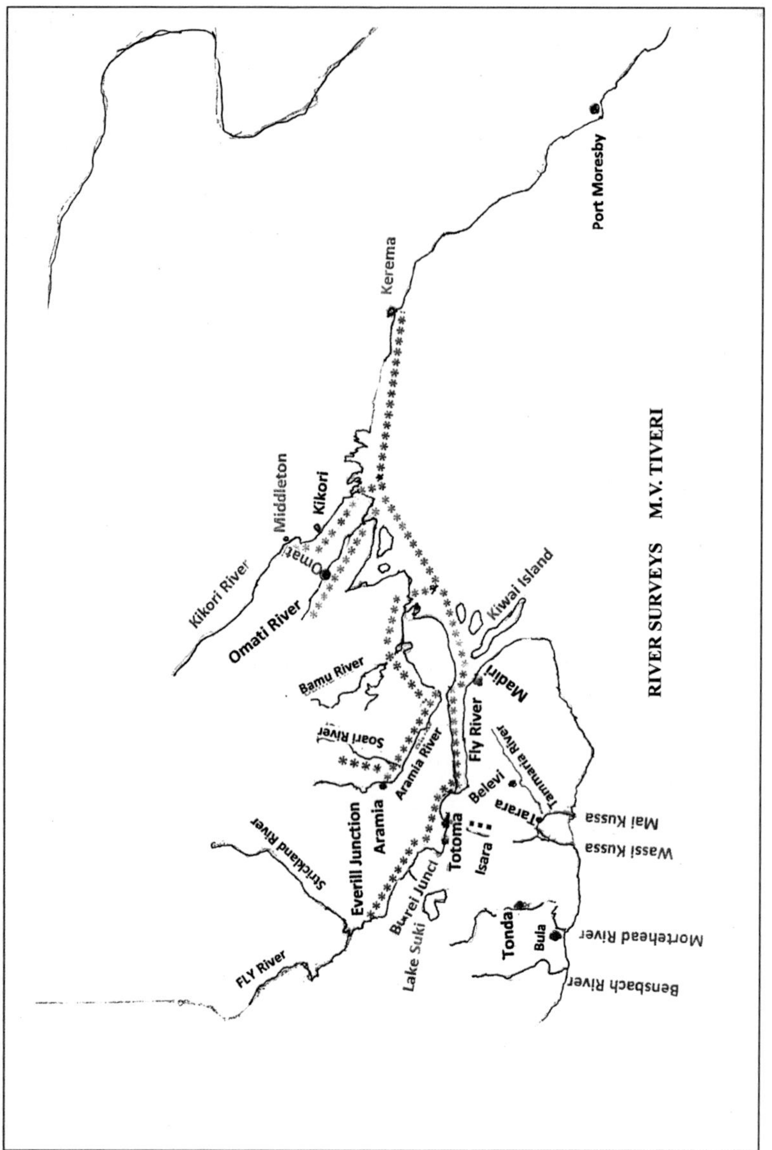

Plot of Captain Baker's river surveys in *M.V. Tiveri*

John Senior, an unknown assistant and carrier line, somewhere in Papua

Rick Wilkinson

Chapter 4
Papuan Gulf Rivers Hydrographic Survey

Field Break

The nine days in Port Moresby were spent looking over the town. The two hotels (*the Top Pub and the Snake Pit*) and the WWII airfield at Kila being the main interests. Kila or the Three Mile as it was known was where the U.S Air Force 3rd Bombardment Group operated from when they commuted to war from Charters Towers.

I had met some of the men during the war and had developed an affection for the North American Mitchell B25 bomber *Baby Blitz*. When in Charters Towers *Baby Blitz* was always parked near the unfenced boundary of the base. At lunch time it was always unattended and available for close inspection by an interested schoolboy. Anything in or attached to the plane was sacrosanct. However it was reasonable to souvenir some 50 calibre rounds and clips to assemble a belt with red, black and blue tipped bullets.

Initially it was a surprise to see that all turrets were armed with the blue tipped bullets because our newspapers had criticised the enemy for using explosive bullets.

Unfortunately *Baby Blitz* did not survive the war although pilot Captain Angel did and he returned home to the United States. *Baby Blitz* was destroyed on the ground during a Japanese raid on the Three Mile strip at Kila.

During my stay in Port Moresby I was able to enjoy a night and a few dances at the public service club and was

Author and Jeep on field break in Port Moresby

invited to play baseball for a local team. I played shortstop with the University of Queensland baseball team and it is not surprising that I don't remember anything noteworthy in the three innings I pitched in the Port Moresby competition. As for batting I was hitless just as I was at the dance the night before.

A.P.C. Mess and Dining Hall at Badili, Port Moresby

During my field break I learnt that I was to join retired Royal Navy Captain Baker on the T boat MV Tiveri to be his assistant on river surveys. This vacancy resulted from Captain Baker's Lieutenant Commander offsider having to return to a sick wife in the United Kingdom.

Some of my part-time work experience had been with the hydrographic section of the Queensland Irrigation and Rivers

Converted Fairmile gun boat *M. V.Negera* on the Omati River

WWII Fairmile gun boat

Department. It surely was a case of any port in a storm when I was plucked from the bush and put on to the comfort of Tiveri.

Port Moresby to Omati

Again on board the Catalina *Isand Chieftan* in Port Jackson (Port Moresby) on my way to the Omati river where we went aboard MV Negera a converted WWII Fairmile gun boat. I travelled on Negera to the A.P.C. drill site at Omati with Mr Hunter the general manager and a Mr Baker a director. Being attentive to their conversation on the two hour trip did not result in my gaining any inside insight into Oil Search shares.

The Fairmiles were built for the British Navy by Fairmile Marine as a counter to the German E-boats. Capable of 40 knots they were originally equipped with depth charges then with torpedoes and finally as gun boats when they were fitted with a 57 mm gun. They served as lead ships in the invasion of Normandy on D day.

Captain Baker and Tiveri

At Omati I met Captain Edmund Henry Buckingham Baker DSO RN (retired) and joined MV Tiveri where I lived and worked for the next six weeks. We had a bosun who had been released from prison after serving a sentence for drinking methylated spirits. We had three native deckhands. The bosun had been released from prison because he had special knowledge of the Papuan Gulf rivers.

One of the deckhands had served on a Burns Philp ship and had been to Sydney on one voyage. The other two had worked on APC boats that carried supplies from Port Moresby to the base camps in the field. One had worked in a galley and he doubled as a cook of average ability.

'Buck' Baker as he was known in the British Navy had a distinguished war service and was decorated with the DSO for his contribution to the Aegean campaign serving with HMS *Nile*. HMS *Nile* was the Royal Navy command at Alexandria in Egypt. Tradition required that the command had a fleet title because every sailor had to serve on a ship.

When on a clandestine attempt to evacuate troops from the island of Leros Captain Baker was captured and spent the rest of the war as a prisoner of war. He became senior officer in Marlag (naval POW camp) Nord, at Tarmstadt near Bremen in Germany, when the original and more senior Royal Navy Captain was killed during a United States Army AIR Force bombing raid on the camp.

British and Polish sailors were imprisoned in the camp.. This Polish experience in Malag Nord and on a 150 mile forced march at the end of the war left Captain Baker with an enduring dislike of Poles. His stories and his action on one occasion made me realise that he had some grim memories of his time as a prisoner of war.

Captain Edmund Henry Buckingham 'Buck' Baker D.S.O. R.N.,A.D.C.
Source: Patricia Sheppard

After the war Captain Baker continued to serve in the Navy before he retired in July 1953 having become Navy Aide de Camp to Queen Elizabeth 2. On the 15th of June 1953 he was senior Royal Naval Officer for one section of the British Fleet during the Queen's Review of the British Fleet at Spithead.

Captain Baker's period spent as a prisoner of war had two unfortunate effects upon his career. Being without command he lost seniority but nevertheless his permanent appointment as a Captain was backdated. This had the effect that he did not actually have the nine years as a Captain that showed on his record. As Captain Baker had not advanced to the rank of Admiral in the nominal nine years as a Captain he was required to resign in 1953.

The Royal Navy hydrographic service had only one Admiral and he was the Navy Hydrographer. Captain Baker was appointed Assistant Hydrographer under an officer who would have been junior to him had he not lost service time while a prisoner of war.

When I joined Tiveri I inherited the case of gin that had been provided for the Captain's original assistant. This meant that every day after work the Captain would have two whiskeys and I would have two gins. It was during these sessions that he relaxed and told me stories about his family and of pleasant occasions with Lord Louis Mountbatten in the Med. On a couple occasions he told me that the Poles were *lugubrious bastards*.

During my time in Papua with APC I worked with two seismic parties and one gravity party and while I had had a lot of joy and excitement with these teams my most interesting experience was with Captain Baker on Tiveri. Apart from the life encounter with such a man and the technical education obtained there was the realisation for me of something more important. This was the realisation of the historical significance of the former Assistant Hydrographer Royal Navy, in 1954 following in the wake of other Royal Navy hydrographers Captain Francis Pike Blackwood and

HMS *Indomitable*

Lieutenant Charles B Yule in the HMS *Fly* and their 1845 discovery of the Fly River.

The surveys by Captain Baker of the Fly River, the Omati River and the Kikori River increased the navigation knowledge about these streams in the interest of their future commercial use. This valuable work surely warrants his inclusion in the list of ships' captains who have applied their skills as navigators, as hydrographers and as explorers on the Fly River and the other rivers mentioned in this book. Likewise M.V. Tiveri is entitled to be on the record with HMS *Fly,* Neva, Ellengowan. Merrie England, Bonito, Elevala, Laurabada and the other ships used by these men on their expeditions.

In 1917 Edmund Baker was a seventeen year old midshipman at Scapa Flow on HMS *Indomitable* when the Battle Cruiser was being commissioned.

He was commissioned two years later and from 1920 to 1922 he was at Cambridge University. After graduation he joined the Royal Navy in the hydrographic division. He served on several survey vessels as hydrographer, navigator or executive officer.

In 1930 he was promoted to the rank of Commander and he took his first command as captain of HMS *Kellet* in November 1934. After Kellett he commanded two other survey vessels HMS *Challenger* and HMS *Scott* until April 1940.

From April 1940 he served at The Admiralty (HMS *President*) on the staff of the Director of Combined Operations Sir Roger J.B.Keyes Admiral of the Fleet Air Arm.

From the Combined Operations he was transferred to the Royal Navy Base Liverpool Convoy Section (Headquarters Western approaches HMS *Eaglit*) until 1942 when he went back to sea in command of survey vessel HMS *Endeavour*.

From June 1943 until he was captured he was senior British naval officer in the Aegean theatre reporting directly to Royal Navy Headquarters at Alexandria (HMS *Nile*). We can assume that it was this command office that decided to mount a diversionary raid with a Marines force while he was engaged on a clandestine operation involving an evacuation from the island of Leros in the Mediterranean.He claimed that he would not have been captured had this raid had not been made. As he said “they drew the crabs”

His promotion to the rank of permanent Captain occurred on the thirty first of December 1943 while he was a prisoner of war.

After the war he was with the Admiralty hydrographic department becoming Superintendent of the Charts branch for three years. In 1948 he commanded HMS *Dalrymple* for a year before becoming Assistant Hydrographer of the Royal Navy followed by another year at sea in command of HMS *Cook.*

From January 1953 until July 1953, when he retired, he was Naval ADC to Queen Elizabeth 2. He had been awarded the DSO for service in the Aegean Sea campaign. His investiture at Buckingham Palace took place on the eleventh of December 1945.

The citation reads, "for undaunted courage, determination and endurance in many sweeps against enemy shipping in the Aegean under fire and constant attack from the air, and in maintaining supplies to the islands of Kos and Leros until they fell to superior forces."

Captain Baker apparently was not over-concerned by not becoming Royal Navy Hydrographer which would have earned him a knighthood. This does not surprise me because he was totally without any show of self-importance. People who knew him after he had retired to North Curry in Somerset remember him as a kind and self-deprecating man.

After his two years in Papua Captain Baker returned to his family in North Curry, a small village seven miles from Taunton in Somerset ,to live the life of *a country gentleman.*

He bought a former Fairmile gunboat that he named *Go Venture* that was moored at Fower beside *Idstraddle* owned by the poet Browning.

I joined Captain Baker on Tiveri at Omati and quickly realised that I was *in the navy*. There was no left and right or front and back it was all port and starboard and fore and

Lord Louis Mountbatten

Author and Hugh Tunney (on the left) at the Gresham Hotel. Dublin. Classiebawn Castle is depicted in painting on wall.

aft. This was relaxed over our evening two drinks each when I learnt something of his life at Taunton in Somerset and his family. Captain Baker had many treasured memories of times spent with his friend Lord Louis Mountbatten with whom he had served in the Mediterranean in 1943, and he shared some of these with me on Tiveri

When Mountbatten was assassinated in 1979 he was holidaying at Mullaghmore, Ireland as a guest of Hugh Tunney in Classiebawn Castle.

Classiebawn Castle was completed in 1874 by Lord Palmerston on land acquired during the seventeenth century by his great grandfather Sir John Temple. Lord Palmerston, Prime Minister of the United Kingdom for almost nine years, was the great grandfather of Lady Edwina Ashley, Lord Louis Mountbatten's wife.

Hugh Tunney later bought Classiebawn Castle and the two rooms used by the Mountbattens in 1979 were maintained as they were **in** 1979 and never used again in Hugh Tunney's life.

River Surveys

The day after I boarded Tiveri we relocated at the rock bar on the Omati River and began a survey of that section of the river. The triangulation and the measurements enabled a plot of the river banks and the location of the rock bar hazard. Captain Baker had used this method on a Canadian survey of the coast of Labrador.

On the Omati we erected stations along the banks and placed buoys anchored in the river. At the turn of the tide Tiveri with echo sounder recording depths cruised along the line of buoys. When we came to a buoy the captain stamped his foot and he and I made simultaneous readings of the appropriate bank stations with a sextant. The chart of this survey that Captain Baker drew was a thing of beauty.

No doubt as a second observer I was useful during this survey but I soon realised that I was more useful with my native labour experience. Captain Baker did not understand his crew and his crew did not understand him. This was highlighted during the placing of the buoys in the river.

Captain Baker in *punt dinghy* placing marker bouys in the Omati River

M.V. Tiveri deck hands making trig station beacons in ***bomb scow***

Landing barge *Guba* and *M.V. Tiveri* at Omati wharf, Omati River

M.V. Tiveri assisting *M.V. Gabuna* to berth at Omati, Omati River

Red Cedar logs at Middletown sawmill on Kikori River

Break down saw at Middletown sawmill

Three man bench saw at Middletown sawmill

The survey began when the row boat (*punt dinghy*) left Tiveri with the Captain at the oars two deckhands and a load of buoys on board. When all the buoys had been set in their planned locations in a line along the river the party began their upstream return to Tiveri with Captain Baker rowing.

When he came alongside the Captain called "throw me the *paynter*" but the deck-hand just looked at him and did not throw him a rope as requested. As he drifted downstream the Captain kept calling for the *paynter* getting quite a distance from Tiveri. I assumed my first command and ordered the bosun to start up Tiveri to pick up the skipper. As usual after any such incident the Captain made no comment afterwards.

Considering that the boys had been painting tide boards the previous day the confusion with the word "painter" can be understood.

Captain Baker never talked about his time as a prisoner of war but on a couple of occasions ,as previously mentioned, he told me that "Poles were lugubrious bastards". He illustrated his own belief in this prejudice one evening at Kikori.

We had accepted an invitation to have dinner with Doctor Zec who was in charge of the Administration Hospital at Kikori. After an excellent meal we moved to the lounge for conversation and drinks. For me it was especially enjoyable to have a couple of cold beers instead of two gins.

Everything was going great until the doctor said "do you know Captain Baker that I am Polish?" Captain Baker lent towards Doctor Zec and almost in a shout said "you are a what?". The doctor said " a Pole". Immediately Captain Baker stood up turned to me and said "back to Tiveri, Tunny" and he turned and we left. No thanks for the dinner and no goodbye as we went. Naturally Tunny (that was how he always addressed me) put down his half glass of cold beer and did what he was told to do.

We were at Kikori measuring and erecting tide level gauges on the Kikori River. This required a trip to Middletown where the Middleton brothers operated the APC sawmill. They supplied the material required for the gauges we erected.

M.V. Tiveri and punt dinghy at Kikori. Bosun at the stern

M.V.Tveri deck hand with river shark

Aerial view of Government Administration centre at Kikori, Kikori River

Kikori government station children watch action on *M.V. Tiveri*

The rivers flowing into the Gulf of Papua experience what are known as 'bores'. These are the 'standing waves' that occur when the rising tide meets the river near its mouth. A bore in the Fly River can be nearly a metre high. And can travel miles upstream. In 1935 when Hides was taking his seriously ill companion to Daru he lost his canoes at Totoma (about 100 miles from the mouth of the Fly Rive) to an unexpected bore.

One night Tiveri was hit by a bore and I awoke to see what I thought was the dynamite store drifting past me. We were dragging the anchor and the activity on the boat made me realise that we had a problem. We were heading downstream stern first towards the sea.

Captain Baker decided that we should free the anchor and return to our usual anchored location beside the dynamite store. This made sense as all ships using the Omati knew where we normally dropped anchor without lights and clear of the rock bar. All we had to do was get away from the snag.

With the bosun at the wheel and the Captain and one deckhand up front we began a routine of going forward and backwards. This was done by the Captain shouting "ahead" and then if we were not free he would shout "astern". At each command he shone his powerful flashlight in the bosun's face and observed him.

Unfortunately after probably fifteen minutes we were still snagged and our skipper was visibly angry. He set off from the starboard side towards port to get to the bosun. I thought that he was going to hit the bosun with the torch because we did not always go in the direction commanded or sometimes it was a bit delayed.

Fate intervened when the deckhand removed the hatch over the anchor chain locker just as Captain Baker was about to step on it. Down he went one leg full length into the locker. I thought he is going to kill someone but no he got up and with head down he kept repeating "I'm a silly old bugger" before telling the bosun "engine off". As usual he never made any comment after this incident. In the morning we got free quickly without any problem.

My last survey with Captain Baker and M.V. Tiveri, before transferring to the Gravity Party on the Wassi Kussa, was a sounding traverse up the Fly River. The Fly River is Australasia's largest river and one of the largest rivers in the world. The bed of the Fly was clear of concealed navigation hazards except for a large tree embedded in the muddy bottom. Well under water pointing upstream at an angle of forty five degrees. A stick of gelignite would set it free to go to sea with all the other logs and trees that were the main hazard in the river. Sometimes so much of the bank would slip into the river that a tree still vertical would float along.

For me Fly River survey was a nostalgic return to places I had come to know when I was with Seismic Two. Burei Creek, Isura River, Suki Creek, D'Albertis Island, Kiwai Island, Madiri, Totoma and Redbank.

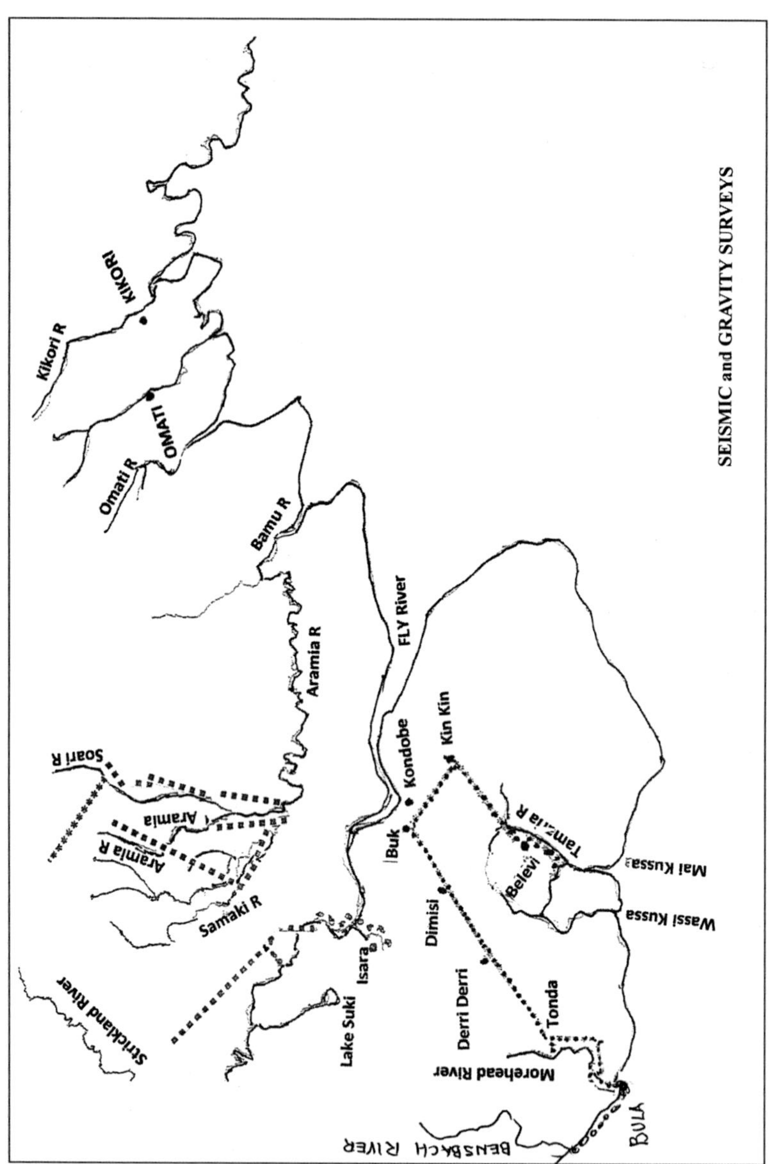

Plot of the author's Seismic and Gravity Surveys

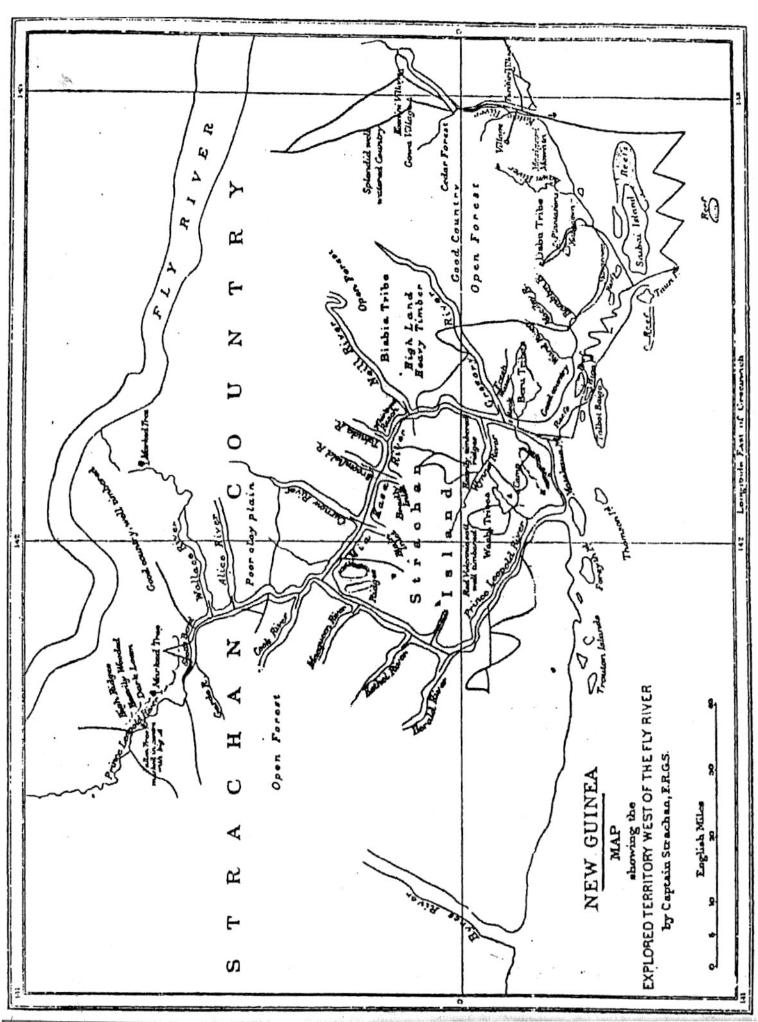

Captain Strachan's map of the area west of the Fly River

Autoloading Molens 57mm gun on Fairmile D boat during WWII.

Chapter 5
South of The Fly River Gravity Survey

Tarara

After the Fly River survey in Tiveri I learnt that I was going to the Gravity Survey Party at Tarara to replace a surveyor who had resigned with a medical problem.

Once again I was back on-board the Island Chieftain this time taking off from the Kikori River and alighting on the Wassi Kussa where Tarara the base camp for the A.P.C. gravity party was located.

Like Seismic Two the Gravity Survey Party was a small group not having the numbers and support structure that Seismic One had. However the accommodation especially the mess, kitchen and recreation area had obviously been built for a large organisation in the past.

My new personal boy was named Morowai and the 'boy line' of 28 men and boys were all Kiwai Islanders. The leader

Catalina flying boat VH EBC *Island Chieftain* at Port Moresby

of the line was Emalio who never failed to perform to a high standard.

After two days at Tarara it was off by bomb scow to the Tamaria River, a tributary of the Mai Kussa. After finding where the river and our survey line met we loaded up and walked into the village of Belevi.

Gravity surveys do not require a straight line with shot points and geophone stations at regular measured intervals so the task was easier as we mostly followed the tracks between the villages.

In less than three weeks we surveyed from Belevi, through Kondobe, Kin Kin to Buk from where we walked back to Tarara. We completed this survey in less than three weeks, being able to survey between three and five miles each day. On one occasion in our enthusiasm I continued surveying

Personal boy Morowai at Tarara

Flying foxes at junction of the Mai Kussa and the Tarama River

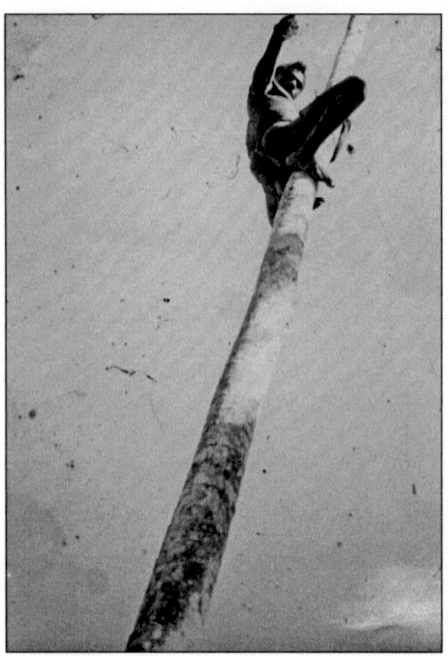

Rigging radio aerial for broadcast schedule with base camp

Kiwai Islander with *Cus Cus*

Author on village track between Kin Kin and Belevi

Village head man welcomes survey team to Kin Kin

until last light knowing that we were getting closer to our next camp, already established ahead of the survey.

Emaiio must have been concerned because we had not stopped work for very long when we were met by one of the team, carrying our faithful Coleman lamp, and he led us to the camp.

Our walk back to Tarara, after we had completed the survey, followed some overnight rain, that had made the track treacherously slippery. It started as a matter for concern when the taubada slipped and crashed to the ground for the first time. When it seemed that just about everybody had slipped and gone down it became a hilarious farce. I did not enjoy the walk and I did not join in the hilarity. After the polite concern for my welfare when I first fell it became great fun for the boys when I fell a few more times. The Coleman lamp carrier never fell so at least we were able to follow the track.

Trading and Village Life

Being a few days ahead of schedule and after having pushed the team hard for most days I decided we had earned a rest. I enjoyed the comfort of village life in the rest house set aside at Buk for the government's patrol officers. The boys were able to use up the excess food loads and enjoy a dance and some socialising with the locals.

At Buk I had my first experience with village trading and with requests for help to meet some needs or medical problems that a couple of the village people brought to me. All my previous surveys had been in uninhabited areas and I had never previously spent a day and a night in a village.

I still have regrets over a request I received for sewing cotton in exchange for a paw paw. I had a full reel of cotton and I rolled off what I now know was a pathetic offering mainly a result of my impatience. The decent thing to do would have been to have given the woman the full reel. I will never forget that afternoon.

One medical problem brought to me was a little girl, probably eighteen months old, with a large infected area on her buttock. I thought it was some ulcer-type infection from an insect bite or a scratch. All I had was a bottle of *brilliant green* which I assume was some penicillin-type powder dissolved in methylated spirits. I knew from use on my own scratches that it stung and the poor little mite cried when I painted the area. I showed more sense on this occasion because I left the bottle with the mother. Patrol officers are trained and more experienced in helping with cases like this. I hope one visited Buk shortly after my stay there.

In my next survey I met an outstanding Papuan lad named Joseph who had been educated at the Sacred Heart Mission on Yule Island. Joseph was one of the gravity party driver mechanics. He had driven out to Derri Derri in a Land Rover to bring me back to Tarara after we had completed the survey.

He was a friendly well-spoken young man who had the Papuan skill with different languages. In Joseph's case he not

Mai Kussa and Wassi Kussa junction at Strachan Island at Tarara

Gravity party mess and dining hall at Tarara on the Wassi Kussa

Kiwai Island survey team boys near Tonda

Authors *donga* at Gravity survey base camp, Tarara, Wassi Kussa

only spoke the Kiwai language but his Engliish was correct and fluent.

More interesting was his ability to read and write French. He corresponded with a French priest who had returned to France after a period on Yule Island. I quickly realised that my B in Junior French was inadequate.

He played guitar reasonably well and I was satisfied that I had held my own in our *You Are My Sunshine* duet. I could not say the same when he wanted to discuss his share portfolio.

The eight hour drive back to Tarara was exciting, as the bush timber bridges over the creeks all showed signs of fire damage and each crossing was a gamble. Joseph assured me that they were alright when he drove out to get me so they would be alright on the way back. We arrived in Tarara at about eight pm and quite soon after arriving safely, much relieved I had a cold beer to celebrate.

Tarara to Tonda to Bula

Before going on this survey I had a meeting with an official who I assumed was from the Australian Department of Foreign Affairs. He spent a long time with me over morning tea and he impressed on me that I must not cross the border into Dutch New Guinea, stressing the dangers of doing so. There were tensions in this area and apparently an Australian yacht and its crew were being held at Merauke which was not far from the border. This was timely advice for I had been thinking of walking on to Merauke at the end of the survey.

Equipped with a map of an earlier seismic survey, I did not expect any problems on the three day walk from Tarara to Tonda on the Morehead River. I expected that the old shot point blast holes would have collected sufficient water for our needs before we got to the Morehead River.

Unfortunately, although we were on the map's survey line there were no shot point blast holes and so no easy water. With such a large team I had to send boys back to a creek twice with four gallon drums. However on the third day the boys who had wandered away from our survey line, looking for pigs, came back with the news that a half a mile to the north there was a shot point blast hole half full of water.

There were two survey lines and only one had been shot and recorded by the geophysicists. We were travelling along the one that had not been shot. I later found out that to speed up the survey two surveyors had previously been used. One had started at the west end and the other at the east end. Unfortunately not only did they not meet but they had passed each other and had kept going for some miles.

As we were now sharing our water supply with the wild pigs we had to boil all our water but that was better than carrying four gallon drums of water more than five miles.

As would be expected it rained on the next day and we again fell victims to the survey lines error. Our map showed just the one crossing of the river so after unloading we let the bomb scow go off on an inspection jaunt upstream. That was a mistake because after we had travelled a little over a mile we hit the river again and had to wait for the bomb scow to return. That was when the rain came and as we had no cover, we just stood and looked and listened. I must have looked sad, no raincoat soaked to the skin and not able to smoke, because one of the youngest of the team, who had been leaning against a tall skinny paper bark tree, one with very few branches and hardly any leaves, came over to me and said *"taubada you can have my tree"*. That moment of powerful emotion made the two hour wait for the bomb scow much easier. I patted him on the shoulder and told him that I was alright, but I now realise that had I accepted his offer I would have made him very happy.

We crossed the Morehead River from the deserted village of Tonda and when we got to the west bank I was able to establish a comfortable camp with good supplies and radio contact with Tarara. From this camp and with use of the bomb scow I was able to connect the parallel survey lines and survey the Morehead River to its mouth at Bula.

Bula to Bensbach River

Bula is a village, situated on the coast near the mouth of the Morehead River, with a small population and good gardens growing coconuts and paw-paws. During my stay there they made very few requests for help and it was a friendly and happy village. Our Kiwais joined them in a sing-sing and

Water supply in old seismic survey shot point blast hole

Bomb scow delivering equipment and supplies to Morehead River camp

Bula village woman tidying up the village

Bula village child

dance on the first night while I relaxed in the patrol officer's rest house.

After we transferred camp to Bula the bomb scow was released and it returned to the Seismic One base above Gumba near Rouku about 60 miles up the Morehead River. The next morning we organised the individual loads and set out for the beach on foot on our way to the Bensbach River.

On the way to the beach I had a close call when crossing a fast flowing creek that ran into the sea. Surprised by the force of the flow I was swept off my feet and on my way to the sea. Fortunately, I was upstream of two of my Kiwai team who grabbed me in time. When we got to the beach Emalio the team leader arranged for two coconuts to be delivered to us. We sat down and had a talk about the survey and how long we would be away from the base camp. I treasure the photograph that I had the good sense to organise. Emalio was a man whom I grew to know and appreciate as someone with character and loyalty you would not often meet. We became good friends. The respect that he enjoyed from the team was always evident and showed in the way they answered every call and put up with some trying challenges.

One such occasion was when I had to make an unscheduled re-location of our camp after one of the boys was injured chasing a shark in the shallows at low tide. Normally there were three or more boys working together on the one shark and at least two sharp sticks would skewer the shark, and a bush knife would end the contest. On this occasion the victim was in front of his mates and the one stick did not prevent the shark from attacking him and separating most of the heel part from the sole of his right foot.

This happened at the one and only beach between the Morehead and Bensbach Rivers. The tide was out and it was an opportunity to get some seafood. There were many stingrays lazing in small puddles and every now and then a small school of sharks would cruise by. The Kiwais were expert in the sea environment and I was happy just to watch. Chasing a crocodile as one of a team is alright but a shark in the water is too dangerous.

The injured boy was in no state to walk, so Emalio took the team back to pack up the camp and bring everything up to the beach site where I waited with the patient. I had a problem being without the medical kit that would have contained some shell dressings and tablets for the *boy's* pain. All I could do was tie his foot together with handkerchiefs and share my tin of Craven A's with him. I would start each day with a round tin of Craven A's with 50 cigarettes in my shirt pocket and refill it at bedtime for the next day. By the time Emalio got back with the camp we had only a few cigarettes left. It had been a long day and part of a night before our faithful Coleman lamp was seen blinking through the mangroves in the distance.

The injured boy settled down without complaining and we sat side by side for about eight hours talking while awaiting the return of the team. I had to tell him why we were out in the bush looking for oil when there were drums

Author during Tonda to Bula survey of the Morehead River

Author's Morehead River camp. Chairs, table etc. from Bomb scow

Kiwai Islander survey team on Morehead River in a Bomb scow

Bula village viewed from Morehead River mouth

Patrol Officer's guest house at Bula village

Bula village viewed from Patrol Officer's guest house

Radio schedule from beach between Morehead to Bensbach Rivers

Survey camp at beach between Morehead and Bensbach Rivers

of it back at Tarara. Explaining what dust was proved to be a bit difficult and I think he thought that I didn't know either.

It would have been seven or eight o'clock when they got back and they had travelled with the tide in and probably only able to start the return journey when the high tide had started to recede. They would have had extra loads to carry because it included all the camp gear and they would have been in the water for at least three hours. This was an effort above and beyond anything I could have expected from any group that I have ever worked with, then or since. The shorter ones were up to their chests and they all would have known they were in shark infested waters on the fringe of the mangroves. Not long after they arrived I had a bed, a tent and a fire prepared for me,before their own camp and meal was ready..

Earlier on this coast survey I had acted like an intrepid explorer, out front, leading my loyal line of carriers into the unknown. This delusion ended the afternoon I came around a small mangrove peninsula to be met by three shark fins in V formation coming towards me. Happily when I stopped they turned away. From that time on I never travelled in the water, always waiting for low tide. Intrepid yes, brave no.

That deserted village beach camp site was our last camp, commuting to work from what was a comfortable and really the only practical location. Travel along the coast became gradually more difficult as we got closer to the Bensbach River. Eventually the quick condition of the silty sand meant that at each step my leg would sink to well above the knee and before the next step I had to pull my leg slowly up and slide it sideways forward.

Survival became the question and conditions were so difficult I decided that the pipe we had been given to mark the border would not be located on the coast but inland on firm ground. We cut a short *dala* through the mangroves to a suitable spot where we planted the pipe and I recorded the location.

Escape dala through mangroves at Bensbach River

Bensbach River distributary

Kiwai Islanders

My team on this survey to the Bensbach River were all Kiwai Islanders and they came from various villages located on Kiwai Island situated in the mouth of the Fly River, and except for its coastal fringes the island is mainly flooded mud plains of swamps and savannah. The island is about sixty kilometres long.

It is thought that the Kiwais migrated from the upper Fly River regions. They are good fishermen and excellent boat crew. The bosun on the M.V. Tiveri was a Kiwai man with extensive experience and knowledge of the Fly and the Kikori River deltas and their many entrances.

Historians when discussing the Kiwai Islanders sometimes comment on the fact that where sago is plentiful and water transport is easy and available it is usual to find headhunting.

It was certainly true with the Kiwais, who believed that fertility was promoted by taking life and that bad spiritual forces were reduced by taking heads. Once taken these heads were kept as trophies.

The Kiwais lived in long-houses, some as long as 150 metres, and these were the focus of ceremonials and feasting. On those occasions the villagers would come together for many weeks.

One ceremony before a headhunting expedition was the sacrifice of a wild boar. This was thought to make the men *hot for blood.* They targeted the inland trans-Fly bushmen and the Gogodalas to create life by taking life violently.

Emalio the leader of my Kiwai team on the Morehead – Bensbach survey was old enough to have witnessed and probably to have taken part in some of these ceremonies.

In 1954 these practices were things of the past, although, occasionally, violence reappeared. The murder of two police officers at Telefomin in 1953 was one instance. Telefomin had been first visited in 1928 and a police post established there in 1948. Jack Hides and Jim O'Malley were attacked during their exploratory patrol through the Papuan interior in 1935. On that expedition thirty two villagers were killed in skirmishes. These ambushes and battles were often revenge for the looting in the villages or after some stealing

Fly River (Suki Villager) head hunter and trophy

Source: R.S.Gilbert

from the gardens by the explorers who were regarded simply as intruders.

Bensbach to Bula to Tarara

When the Bensbach survey was completed we returned to our beach camp and made plans for an early start back to Bula in the morning. We left at 5 am, well before low tide, an only made four miles in four hours. We were forced to stop by the ferocity of the mosquitoes being required to travel close to the mangroves by the tide.

I was alright after a liberal application of dibutyl thallial but there was not enough for the boys who resorted to covering their bodies with mud or wrapping themselves in blankets. With the tide fully out we were able to walk the remaining twenty odd miles to Bula, well clear of the mangroves and the mosquitoes. I completed this walk bare-footed after one shoe came off in the mud when we were having trouble near the Bensbach River and the second one fell to pieces on the walk out.

Some years later, I read that Michael Rockefeller had gone missing after he had attempted to swim ashore from his upturned canoe. He had been travelling a bit west of, and not far from, where we had been struggling earlier. Had he survived the sharks and the stingrays he would have crawled onto an almost impossible quicksand beach and hordes of mosquitoes. He had no chance.

Kiwai hunters with wild pig

Author's second shoe after first shoe was lost, stuck in the beach mud

Stingray collected from low tide pool at,deserted village, beach camp

Shark speared at low tide at, deserted village, beach survey camp

Kiwai team at Bula after return from Bensbach River

At Bula we boarded the Seismic One bomb scow and travelled upstream to the old survey line crossing of the Morehead River, we then walked back to Tarara. After a few days rest we did the first of several short surveys originating from the Mai Kussa, north of Tarara before ending my time with Australasian Petroleum.

I had a Maths 2 exam to pass and decided to return early to Brisbane for a bit of study to be certain of passing.

Again a Catalina trip to Port Moresby and except for a delay at the airport, when a forklift tine punctured the fuselage of my plane while loading freight, my time as a taubada ended without any fuss. I was somewhat lighter in weight and urgently in need of a haircut but in good health and looking forward to being a student again.

When I left Papua it was not to get away but rather to meet my forthcoming exam commitment in Brisbane. I had enjoyed every experience, especially when out on survey, probably because I was suited to be what Sir Hubert Murray and James Sinclair called an *outside man.* Had it been possible I would have been happy to stay longer.

Gravity party farewell from Tarara jetty on the Wassi Kussa

Trans Australian Airways Skymaster at Jackson's, Port Moresby

Chapter 6
History of The Fly River The Men and The Ships

The geographical relationship between the Fly River and Papua invites comparisons with the Mississippi in the United States, the Amazon in South America, the Nile in Egypt and the Rhine in Europe.

Probably more inviting is the idea to research and record the history of the surveys and expeditions associated with the Fly.

The following summary while not a complete history is a record of the ships and the men who explored or who used the Fly River as the natural and most convenient route to go into the inland of Papua to discover and publicise previously unknown people and places.

The first man to recognise the existence of the Fly was Captain Francis Blackwood in HMS *Fly* in 1845. The ships and leaders that followed him were:

- Reverend Samuel Macfarlane in Ellengowan 1875
- Luigi Maria D'Albertis in Neva 1875

- Captain Henry Everill in Bonito, 1885
- Sir William MacGregor in Merrie England 1889/90
- Sir Hubert Murray 1914
- Charles Karius and Ivan Champion in Elevala 1927
- Jack Hides and James O'Malley in Laurabada 1935
- Jack Hides and David Lyall in Robin S. and Peter Pan, 1937

In 1954 Captain Baker in M.V. Tiveri, equipped with echo sounding equipment, surveyed the river to record an accurate assessment of depths and hazards.

HMS FLY
Captain Francis Price Blackwood RN

The Fly was a fully rigged Orestes class sloop 38.5 metres long on the gun deck. She had a complement of 120 and was armed with sixteen 32 pounder cannonades and two 9 pounder bow 'chasers'. She was launched at Pembroke dockyard on the 25th of August 1831 and commissioned at Plymouth on the 29th of January 1832.

After service on the North American and the West Indian Station HMS *Fly* was 'paid off' in 1840. She returned to service in 1841 as a Royal Navy survey vessel when commissioned under Captain Francis Price Blackwood to survey the Torres Strait in company with the cutter Brambles. It was during this survey that Captain Blackwood observed the large volume of fresh water flowing into the Gulf of Papua. He recognised the existence of a large river

Painting of HMS *Fly*

Source: Wikipedia

draining the interior of the country and named the river the Fly.

Blackwood did not travel up the Fly River, concentrating his survey on the Kikori delta area. Others on the Fly were Lieutenant Charles B. Yule and the Mate David Aird. On a later survey Yule and Aird were killed by local villagers and they are remembered on the map of Papua by Yule Island , the Aird River and Mount Aird .

After a second survey period in Australian and New Zealand waters Fly was 'paid off' again in December 1851 and became a coal hulk until broken up in 1903.

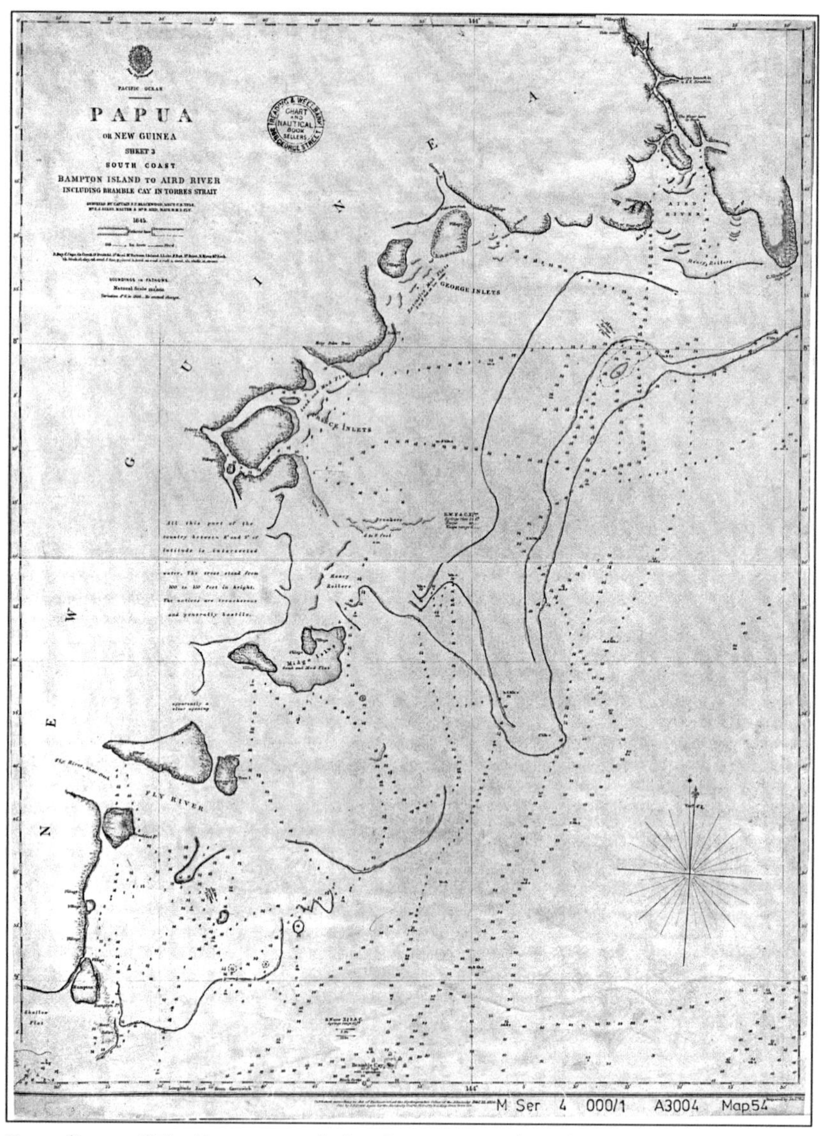

Soundings of Fly River mouth by Captain Blackwod R.N. in HMS *Fly*

Source: N.S.W. State Library

Ellengowan
Reverend Samuel Macfarlane

Ellengowan a single screw steamer displacing 87 tons was donated to the London Missionary Society by a Mrs Baxter and was named after that lady's home in Scotland. The Reverend Samuel Macfarlane an LMS missionary explored the Fly River in Ellengowan looking for suitable sites for LMS mission stations.

His first expedition probably resulting from Captain Blackwood's report, was a voyage up the Mia Kussa that he named the Baxter. He accurately reported that this could not be the big river reported by Blackwood. Macfarlane had steamed up the Mia Kussa for 67 miles in Ellengowan and then continued for a further 24 miles under sail.

Later that year he entered the Fly River and steamed up the Fly for a distance of 150 miles over three days. At that distance from the mouth of the river he reported a depth of 17 fathoms (102 feet) and a river width of one mile. This was indeed Blackwood's Fly River. Called the Fly by Blackwood in 1845 it was not officially named until 1876 when it was listed in a House of Commons White Paper.

Macfarlane left Somerset, at the tip of Cape York, in the Ellengowan on the 29th of November 1875 and reached the mouth of the Fly on the 6th of December. The speed of the river's flow restricted progress to fifteen miles a day, and the voyage of 150 miles up the Fly took until the 18th of December when they turned back after repairing a broken propeller shaft.

They were threatened on one occasion by armed villagers in twenty one canoes who took cover after one of the passengers D'Albertis exploded dynamite ahead of them. These were probably villagers from Adogostia (50 miles from the mouth of the Fly River) where the Macfarlane party had previously inspected a 150 yard long boy house adorned with heads that had been preserved intact.

Macfarlane did not find any suitable high ground on which he could establish a mission. He reported that except for some high red banks it was open country, dead level and perfect swamp with occasional clumps of bamboo.

Passengers on the Ellengowan on this 1875 expedition were Italian naturalist Luigi Maria D'Albertis and Henry Marjoribanks Chester a Queensland Government Police Magistrate stationed at Somerset on the northern tip of the State at Somerset

In April 1883 Chester travelled from Somerset to Yule Island where, as instructed by the Queensland Premier Sir Thomas Macilwraith, he took possession of British New Guinea in the name of her Majesty Queen Victoria. Macilwraith took this initiative to forestall any annexation of the territory by Germany.

For D'Albertis it was the first of three expeditions that he made up the Fly River. He returned the next year with the nine ton 52 foot steam launch Neva.

Reverend Samuel Macfarlane, London Missionary Society

London Missionary Steamer *Ellengowan*

Source: John Goode

Neva
Luigi Maria D'Albertis

The Neva a New South Wales Government ten ton steam pinnace was carried to Thursday Island from where it crossed Torres Strait to enter the Fly River. With only six inches of freeboard amidships it caused D'Albertis and his engineer many worrying moments.

The ship's engineer was Lawrence Hargrave who later became more famous for his pioneering work on the science of flight in heavier than air machines.

It should be noted that the charts drawn by Hargrave and D'Albertis disagreed on some vital detail.

On his first expedition in the Neva D'Albertis became the first known white man to travel the full navigable length of the Fly River. He discovered the Strickland River and its junction with the Fly at what became known as Everill Junction.

Hargrave made only the one expedition with D'Albertis and they had many disagreements. In Hargrave's opinion the collecting of artefacts and even bodies by D'Albertis was more like looting.

D'Albertis later wrote and published an account of his voyages and catalogued his vast collection of birds, plants, weapons, artefacts and human heads and bodies. He was elected as a member of the New South Wales Royal Society in 1877.

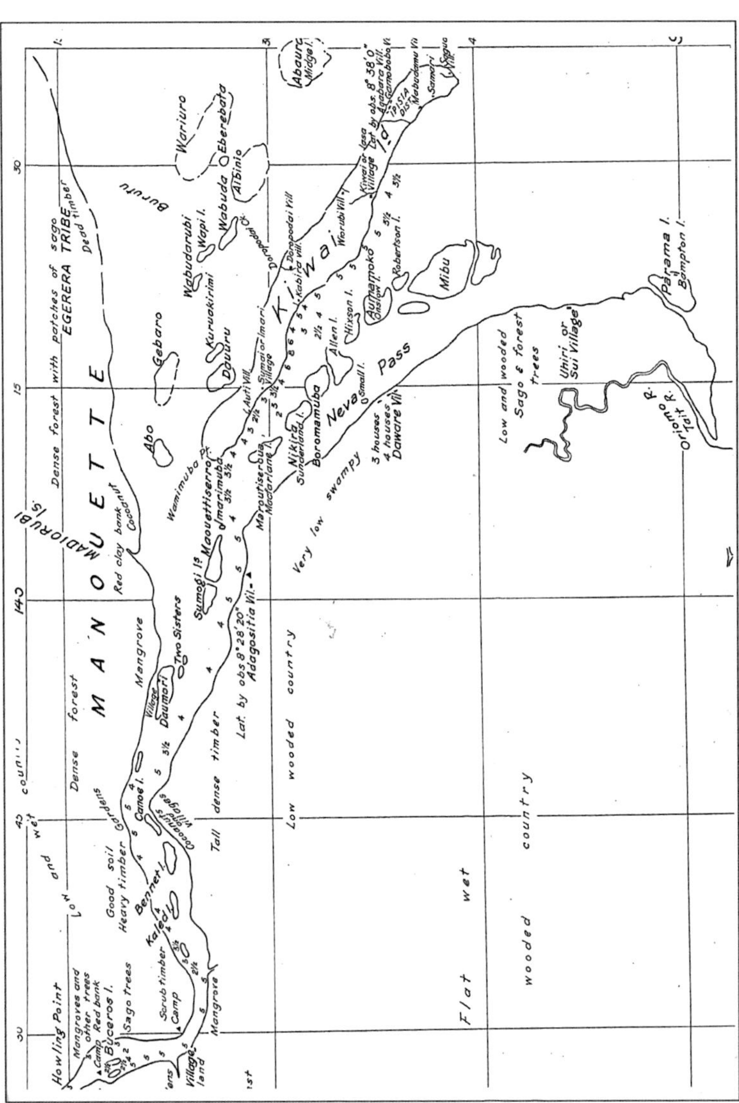

Plot of Macfarlane's expedition up the Fly River in *Ellengowan*

Source: N.S.W. State Library

Luigi Maria D'Albertis, Italian explorer and naturalist

Source: H.J.Gibney - Wikpedia

Henry Marjoribanks Chester, Queensland Government Magistrate

Source: John Goode

Lawrence Hargrave, Australian engineer and aviation pioneer

Source: Amirah Inglis - Wikpedia

New South Wales Government pinnace *Neva*

Source: John Goode

On his second expedition up the Fly River, again in the Neva, D'Albertis visited Kiwai Island and eight days later was at what was then known as Ellengowan Island which is now almost certainly D'Albertis Island today. After 55 days he returned to Kiwai Island having proved that the Fly was navigable for 600 miles.

In 1877 he made his third and final journey up the Fly River.This trip was a disaster and he later had to defend himself against a charge of having murdered one of his crew.

Again in Neva he left Somerset on the 3rd of May 1877 with an Englishman named Preston as his engineer and a crew of ten including some Chinese. One Chinese crewman died after a beating and except for one native the rest of the crew deserted. On his return to Somerset,D.Albertis was found not guilty of murdering the crewman.

D'Albertis was born on the 21st of November 1841 and he joined the Italian general Garibaldi's army when eighteen years old. Born into a rich and influential family he was able to spend a lot of his time living and hunting in the Italian Alpines.

In 1872 he teamed up with the botanist Dr.Beccori and they spent nine months in the north west region of Papua collecting and recording. They collected many Birds of Paradise including some new species. D'Albertis then spent ten months in Sydney and two months in Honolulu before returning to Italy with his collection.

In 1874 he returned to Papua setting up a base at Yule Island from where he travelled into the interior of Papua in that region collecting and recording his discoveries. It was in 1874 that the LMS missionary Samuel Macfarlane began the expansion of the LMS from his base at Somerset. It is not surprising that he met Chester at Somerset and D'Albertis at Yule Island, and this would explain why they were with Macfarlane on the Ellengowan on the voyage up the Fly in 1875 as described earlier.

Luigi Maria D'Albertis was not typical of the explorer naturalists of his time. He did not do quick trips through new country charting and detailing features and nature. He would spend long periods living near the villages using this contact to collect and to learn from the local inhabitants.

Others like Hargrave and Goode describe his behaviour as unacceptable and D'Albertis himself realised that by taking sacred artefacts, weapons, food and even bodies he made himself disliked by the villagers.

He established his control over this threat by assuming an air of invincibility openly kissing the women and giving demonstrations of his power. One of these demonstrations was to challenge the men to penetrate a sheet of iron. After they had broken their spears and destroyed the tips of their arrows he would blow a hole through the sheet of iron with one pistol shot.

He demonstrated how he could burn the sea by lighting some methylated spirits in a sea shell. This, plus dynamite on rockets,and hidden gunpowder ignition trails leading to sticks of dynamite led to acceptance that he was big *fella sorcerer*

His stores included one rifle, four six-shooters, dynamite, 2000 bird shot cartridges and bullets, rockets, fireworks and nine shotguns. On his ship he kept a pet python with his stores to deter his crew from stealing.

The explorers were all intruders and their presence was universally resented by the local villagers. Some were murdered and others in some cases, even missionaries had to resort to killing as defence and for self-protection.

Nevertheless in all the time he lived alone near the villages D'Albertis had only the one confrontation. This happened on Yule Island. Some accounts claim that he was in fact rescued and saved from death on that occasion.

If all the stories about him are true then he can be said to have 'Out Flynned!' Errol Flynn and the future film hero's notoriety in Papua. Before achieving fame in Hollywood Flynn for a short time was a tobacco planter not far from Port Moresby. He established for himself a devil-may care attitude to life but none of his escapades were as dubious as the things said to have been done by D'Albertis.

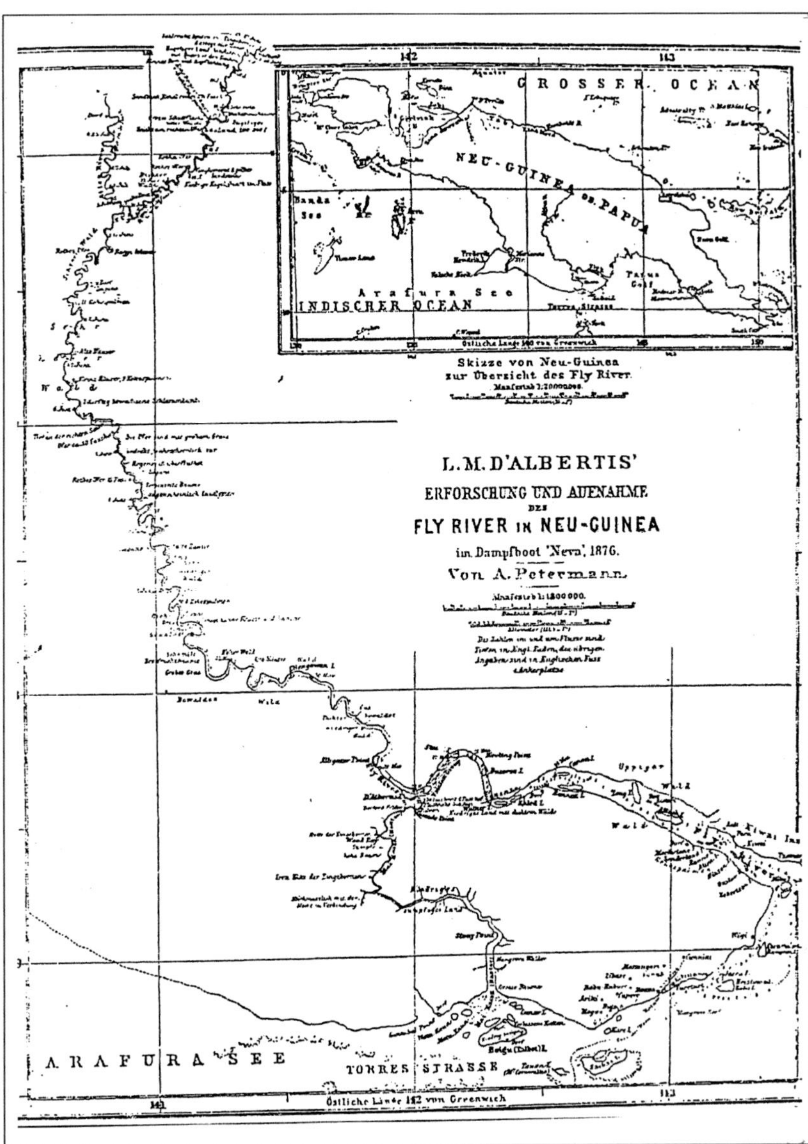

Plot of the D'Albertis expedition up the Fly River in the Neva
Source: N.S.W. State Library

Queensland Government steamship S.S. *Bonito*

Source: Queensland Maritime Museum

John Douglas Englishman, Botanist

Source: R.B.Joyce - Wikpedia

Bonito
Captain Henry Everill

After the 1877 D'Albertis expedition the next important visit to the Fly River was by Master Mariner Captain Henry Charles Everill in 1885. This expedition was under the auspices of the Geographical Society of Australasia. The Queensland Government made the steamship Bonito available for the exploration.

John Douglas the Government Resident and Police Magistrate at Thursday Island accompanied the expedition as far as the Kiwai Island and assisted with the repairs to the Bonito before the Queensland Government ship S.S. Advance towed the Bonito to the mouth of the Fly River.

John Douglas who later became the High Commissioner for British New Guinea was a nephew of John Sholto Douglas the ninth Marquess of Queensberry.

The rules of boxing written by John Graham Chambers had been publicly acknowledged by the Marquess and so the rules have become known as the Queensberry Rules, the code for gentlemanly boxing. The rules were detailed and they described the circumstances that could arise in a bout and how each rule should be applied. For instance rule number five prescribes one situation when the knock out count to ten can commence. It states "that when a man is hanging on the ropes in a helpless state with his toes not touching the ground he shall be considered *down*.

This state of helplessness could be an analogy to the state of affairs in which Oscar Wilde found himself after an ungentlemanly bout with the Marquess of Queensberry. Wilde had sued Queensberry for libel but evidence produced by the defence caused Wilde to withdraw the action. His bankruptcy setback, because of the costs , was compounded by the two years, gaol sentence that he served after the defence sent their evidence to Scotland Yard.

Captain Henry Charles Everill a Master Mariner had been a tobacco plantation manager in Sumatra before being appointed to lead the Geographical Society expedition to explore the Aird River in Papua. But local advice after the Bonito reached Thursday Island caused the plan to be changed to an exploration of the Fly River.

There was a lot of controversy after the expedition returned to Australia. Everill claimed that the expedition had been a success and this claim was supported by the Geographical Society. However The Queenslander newspaper journalist wrote that nothing had been achieved.

The Queenslander printed a story by their special reporter that the Bonito had arrived in Cooktown at 1 pm on Monday the 23rd of November being towed by the SS Alexandria. After three hours in Cooktown the Bonito left for Brisbane still *in tow.*

Initially members of the party were reluctant to discuss the expedition saying that the information obtained belonged to the Geographical Society. However after their *lengthy walk* down the street in Cooktown this reluctance was lost and they told tales that experienced bush men said were unbelievable.

The general opinion in Cooktown was that the whole expedition had been "more or less a failure". One member of the party is quoted as saying "the real reason why the expedition turned back was because they had run out of condensed milk".

Another member of the party claimed that they had come across a mountain that was covered in snow. Captain Everill showed what he called frost bite on his hands. The journalist wrote that these were just ordinary New Guinea sores or what is known to bush men as *Barcoo Rot*

Before Captain Everill in Bonito returned to Thursday Island on Friday the 20th of November 1885 it had been reported that the Bonito expedition members had been massacred by hostile natives. Accordingly a relief party on a fast lugger, the Wild Duck, skippered by Captain Dubbins had already set out, before Bonito reached Thursday Island, to investigate the truth of this story.

At Kiwai Island at the start of the trip up the Fly River Everill had increased the size of their party by recruiting three Papuan villagers as guides and interpreters, but all three deserted on the 9th of August. This was a week after the only brush with natives that the expedition had experienced. It was thought that this incident was why the Papuans had left. When they reached Kiwai the deserting Papuans reported that the Everill expedition had been massacred and this misinformation was then sent to

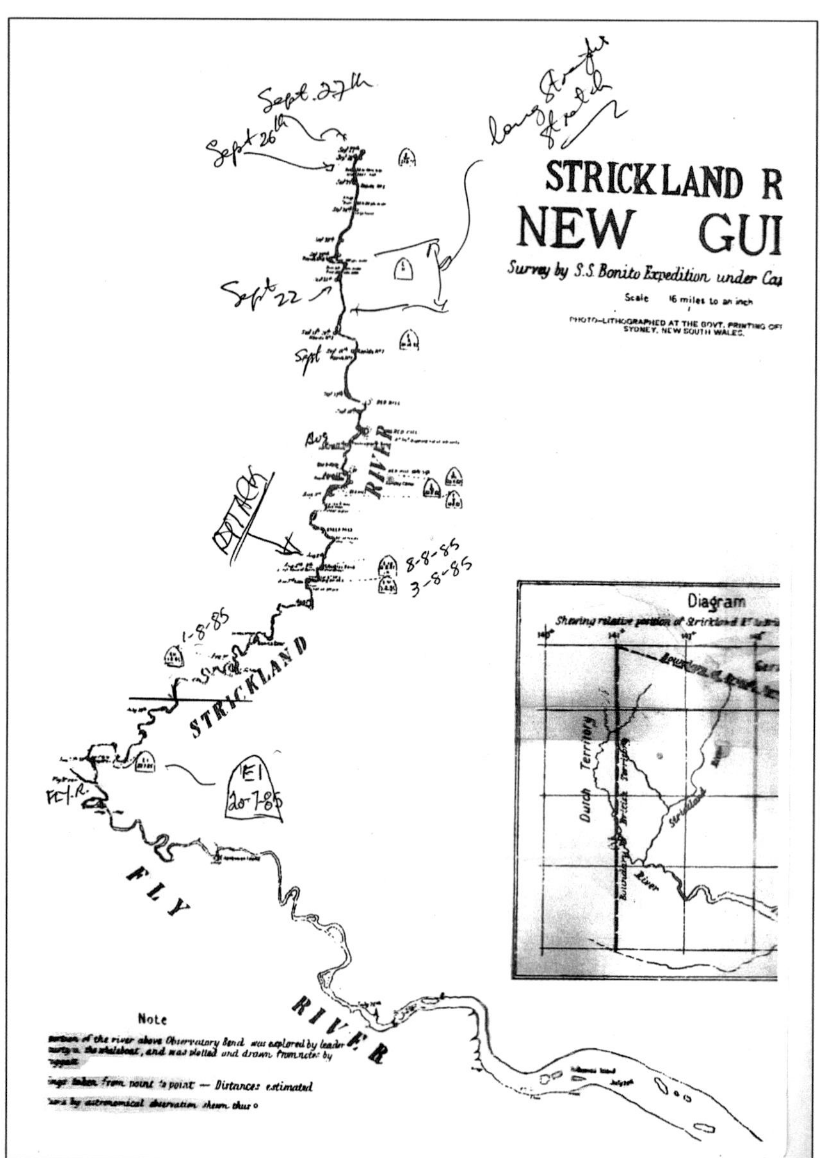

Captain Everill's map of Fly River expedition in S.S. *Bonito*

Source: N.S.W. State Library

Thursday Island. It was three months later that the relief party left Thursday Island.

At Thursday Island Everill was welcomed and entertained by John Douglas which corrects Ivan Champion's later report that Douglas had gone on the expedition with Everill.

There were two published reports of the expedition. Everill wrote one referring to the plot of the journey up the Fly and the Strickland Rivers by surveyor cartographer Mr Senior. Everill travelled up the Strickland in Bonito to its navigable limit. Twelve of the party completed the expedition in a whaleboat to a point 70 miles above were the Bonito was stuck fast.

Everill stressed that the expedition had been conducted on temperance principles without any stimulants and claimed that "any hard work can be performed just as well without alcohol as with it and a daily dose of quinine".

The Queenslander's journalist reported the party's loss of reluctance to speak about the expedition. He claimed that their reluctance to speak had disappeared after their three hours walk down the main street in Cooktown. If the temperance principle was discarded in Cooktown then the changed attitude and the *far-fetched* stories are explained.

Everill's report is detailed and it corresponds with the published plot. Both are based on the daily notes kept by Mr Froggart the team's entomologist. He nominates three thousand specimens as having been collected in contradiction to the two hundred reported in the Queenslander.

In addition to the collecting of specimens done it took during the time the Bonito collecting continued for the two months Bonito was stranded there. With four qualified scientists a photographer and a surveyor in the party the three thousand figure is more credible.

Everill reported that at the conclusion of his voyage north he climbed a seven hundred and fifty foot high hill only to be confronted with another hill, approximately the same height, He made no reference to any snow-covered hill. This suggests that he also may have abandoned temperance at Cooktown.

Bonito was a lot of trouble. It had been towed from Sydney by the Egmont as far as Brisbane and from Brisbane to abreast of Townsville by the Wentworth and from that point to Thursday Island towed by the Alexandria. The seas had been rough and a survey at Thursday Island resulted in extensive repairs that took almost three weeks to complete. Bonito set off for the Fly River on the 14th of July towed by the Advance.

Apart from confirming and plotting several of the locations mentioned by D'Albertis Captain Everill named the Strickland River after Sir Edward Strickland KCB who was the President of the New South Wales Branch of the Geographical Society.

The second report was published by the expedition's botanist William Bauerlen who claims to have collected many samples and specimens. He reports that while the Bonito was bogged for eight weeks and while Everill went further up the Strickland in the whaleboat that collecting and recording continued. His report is mainly a description of the country with detail of the many groundings of Bonito. However it confirms that the expedition was not a total failure.

William Bauerlen confirms that of the many occasions when Bonito was grounded and stranded. Once such grounding lasted for a week and on another occasion the ship was stuck for four days at a place they called Palm Hills. These incidents plus some shorter snagging happened on the way up the river and before the two months stranded at Observatory Bend. Rising waters eventually freed Bonito at the end of October when she was hauled upright after capsizing at anchor.

On the way south another four days were lost at Palm Hills before the speed of the current forced Everill to travel Bonito downstream stern first. This was achieved by operating the engine at a level that gave the ship a speed just below the speed of the river.

Everill does not report this and his description reads "Although time and space does not permit me to detail our homeward journey, I will briefly state that we left Observatory Bend, October 25th, leaving the Malay (Marco Polo) buried there, and the health of the party far from good at that time, safely journeying down the Strickland River with a few adventures. We left Strickland Junction on the 9th of November and the mouth of the Fly on the 18th of November".

Bonito's expeditionary career had certainly been an adventurous one including travelling backwards down the Strickland, sailing across Torres Strait, being beached on a coral reef, being grounded many times on river rock and gravel bars, capsizing and being hauled upright, towed through some wild seas from Sydney to the mouth of the Fly, once filling with water and having to be towed from Thursday Island to Brisbane.

After those experiences it is not surprising that Bonito lost her false keel and one can readily accept the Queenslander's report that "when Bonito passed the S.S. City of Melbourne at 6 o'clock this morning near Cooktown she seemed in a very dilapidated condition."

Apart from the perseverance of the crew the above record says a lot for the quality of work done by her makers, Walkers Shipbuilding at Maryborough in Queensland. It was one of five ships built for the Queensland government in 1887. They were the largest warships built in Australia before Federation.

Merrie England
Sir William MacGregor

Although a qualified and experienced medical graduate Sir William MacGregor came to Papua in 1887 as the administrator of British New Guinea. He already had a background as a Colonial Administrator in the Seychelles and in Mauritius. In Fiji he had served as Colonial Secretary and as acting Governor.

His interest in the problems of labour and his desire to care for the underprivileged population was the reason why he devoted so much time to travel in the furtherance of these ideals.

In 1889/90 he travelled up the Fly River and the Palmer River to report on the resources and the capacity of these areas to support industry and a European population. He left Daru on the 24th of December 1889 in the Merrie England and travelled over 1200 miles in just under six weeks before returning to Kiwai Island on the 2nd of February 1890.

On the 14th of December when travelling north the expedition had been attacked by the Tagota (Totoma) villagers. Strangely enough on the 1st of February on the return voyage they were received peacefully at Tagota.

The Merrie England was able to navigate the Fly to about ten miles north of Tagota from where it returned to Daru. The rest of the expedition was done in the steam launch "Ruby" and two whale boats. The Merrie England had left the expedition at Kiwai and returned to Thursday Island to take the Ruby in tow backto Kiwai.

A chart of the expedition was drawn by Mr Cameron a member of the party and MacGregor made arrangements for the chart to be traced and copies distributed to the Royal Geographical Society branches in England, Scotland, Queensland and New South Wales. During his voyage he named Everill Junction, Mount Blucher and Mount Donaldson.

Sir William MacGregor, Scotchman, doctor and administrator

Steamship Merrie England

Source: James Sinclair

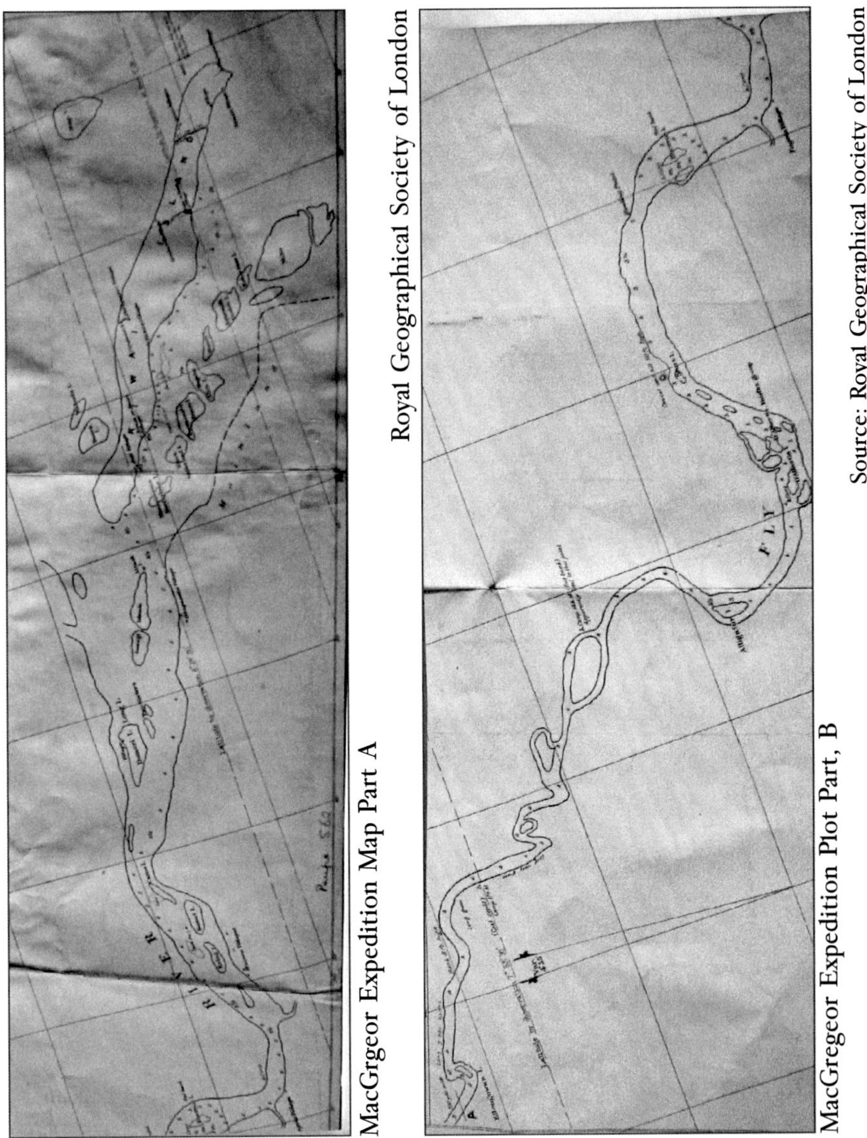

MacGrgeor Expedition Map Part A

Royal Geographical Society of London

MacGregeor Expedition Plot Part, B

Source: Royal Geographical Society of London

Prior to the Fly expedition MacGregor led a team from Port Moresby on the 20th of April 1889 that climbed to the summit of a peak on the Owen Stanley Range. When he reached the summit, 12,500 feet above sea level, on the 11th of June he named the feature Mount Victoria.

After he was appointed Governor in 1895 he continued his promotion of the native Papuans. He backed the appointment of Papuan police officers and encouraged the greater participation of the Papuans in developing plantations and operating gold mining ventures.

He reported that from the mouth of the Fly to Togota there were settled agricultural villages. From Togota to the junction of the Strickland and the Fly at Everill Junction he noted that there was a gap in settlement except for one large village. This would have been the Suki village where the Suki Creek enters the Fly River.

There was a settled tribal village at Everill Junction and another between there and the junction of the Alice River (Ok Tedi). At D'Albertis Junction there were four tribes that MacGregor recognised as more or less nomadic.

He found no traces of precious metals except for traces of gold that was not procurable in payable quantities. He observed stands of Cedar and Malava and small quantities of sago palms.

In 1909 MacGregor was appointed Governor of Queensland after being Governor of Lagos, Nigeria in 1898 and Governor of Newfoundland in 1904. He went into retirement from Queensland in 1909, and died in 1919.

Laurabada
Sir Hubert Murray

Sir John Hubert Murray came to Port Moresby in 1904 as the Chief Justice of British New Guinea. An 1886 Oxford graduate he had been practising as a barrister and occasionaly served in western New South Wales as a prosecutor or as a circuit judge.

His Papuan travel in Laurabada was mostly connected with his duties as Chief Justice and like MacGregor his desire to promote the advancement of the native Papuans.

In addition to his academic ability he was a champion boxer and footballer and had served as an officer in the Boer war. It is not surprising to learn that he considered himself to be one of the *outside men* in Papua and was especially proud of the exploretory achievements of recognised 'Outside Men' like Hides, O'Malley, Champion and Karius.

When he was appointed to the position of British New Guinea Lieutenant-Governor in 1908 his criticisms of several of the serving administration officers led to their dismissal. As a result he acquired many foes among the roughly one thousand white citizens.However he outlived most of his enemies and was recognised for his outstanding contribution to the establishment of Papua when he passed away in office in 1940 at Samurai.

In 1914 when he was Lieutenant-Governor he had travelled in the 30 ton ketch Elevala 35 miles up the Alice River (Ok Tedi) a tributary of the Fly River. He included

Sir Hubert Murray, Australian ,administrator and explorer
Source: H.N. Nelson. Australian Dictionary of Biography

Government Administration steamer Laurabada
Source: Ivan F. Champion

many of his observations during this voyage in his two published books.

Kismet
Sir Rupert Clarke

After Sir Hubert Murray the only significant expeditions were those done by Karius and Champion in 1927 and by Hides and O'Malley in 1935. Both these expeditions were more concerned with opening up the country beyond the Fly and the Strickland. This was the plateau area beyond the difficult limestone mountains that were without much water but with a lot of hostility on the part of the inhabitants.

Sir Rupert Clarke, Australian entrepreneur and politician
Source: R.J.Couthey - Australian Dictionary of Biography

Charles Karius District Magistrate and explorer

Source: Ivan F. Champion

Ivan Champion, Australian, administrator, patrol officer and explorer

Source: Chris Ballard - Australian Dictionary of Biography

Leo Austen in 1922 and Sir Rupert Clarke in 1924 led expeditions but in Clarke's case there is nothing available to reveal what was achieved. Clarke financed and led a survey that was in effect a search for gold. His companions the Pryke brothers, Frank and Dan were experienced gold prospectors and miners but apparently their journey up the Fly River in the yacht Kismet was fruitless.

Clarke born in 1865 was the second Baronet of Rupertswood. Through inheritance he became a pastoralist with large sheep and cattle properties in Queensland and Victoria. As well as being a member of the Victorian Legislative Council he was a true entrepreneur involved in banking, property in the United Kingdom and in Monte Carlo, rubber plantations in New Guinea, picture theatres In Sydney and mining in Coolgardie. He served as a lieutenant in the first World War and was invalided out of the army in 1917. He died in Monte Carlo in 1926.

Elevala
Charles Karius and Ivan Champion

Charles Karius and Ivan Champion grew up as boyhood friends in Port Moresby and together as Patrol Officers they established the Police Camp at Kambisi. They were destined to be the first to cross the New Guinea Island from the south coast through the Fly River and down the Sepik river to the North coast.

This expedition was the idea of Sir Hubert Murray after his own voyage up the Fly and Alice Rivers. The unsuccessful encounters of Leo Austen and W.H. Thompson with the great limestone barrier at the head of the Strickland River led Murray to choose Karius to mount an expedition that would reach the headwaters of the Sepik River. Karius invited Champion to join him on the journey.

The first and unsuccessful attempt left Daru with eleven police and 37 Fly River carriers on the 8th of December 1926. They established a base camp on the Fly River 625 miles from Daru from which Karius and Champion tried separate

Papua New Guinea Administration launch *M.V. Elevela*

Source: Ivan F. Champion

paths to go north across the limestone barrier. They both failed and returned to Daru.

Karius reached Daru on the 10th of June 1927 by way of the Strickland River. Champion did not get back to Daru until the 13th of July 1927. Champion had made progress in that he had reached the source of the Fly River and had made contact with the Bolivip people who knew a way across the limestone barrier.

This was the route followed by Karius and Champion on their second attempt. With six police, a cook and 36 Ferguson Island carriers they left Daru on the 7th of September 1927 and reached Bolivip on the 25th of

Jack Hides on left and David Lyall patrol officers and explorers.
Source: James Sinclair

November. On the 1st of December they stood on a grassy knoll 7,150 feet above sea level and looked down the Sepik Valley and the Takin River the headwaters of the Sepik River.

After a week they descended into the valley and reached the furthermost point that the Germans had reached up the Sepik River, during their occupancy of this part of New Guinea before the first World War.. Champion was suffering from an infected knee and was being carried on a stretcher.

On the 24th of December Karius and three policemen were confronted by a group of natives, but they threw down their arms when challenged. One of their carriers died on the1 18th of January a day before they set off by raft down the Sepik.

When still miles from the mouth of the Sepik they were surprised after rounding a bend in the river to see the Elevala under Captain Ritchie waiting for them.

Elevala was sunk by the Japanese in WWII.

Laurabada
Jack Hides and James O'Malley

The last of the major surveys from the Fly River was done in 1935 by Jack Hides the Administration Registered Magistrate at Misima and Patrol Officer James O'Malley. Sir Hubert Murray described this patrol into the great Papuan Plateau as the "most difficult and dangerous ever conducted in Papua".

Sailing from Port Moresby in the Laurabada they recruited thirteen Goaribari carriers from the Auma village. At Kikori thirteen more carriers and two prisoners were added to the party.

At Daru they loaded the Elevala with sago, sugar cane, coconuts and four light cedar dugout canoes. The expedition left Daru on the 2nd of January 1935.

Elevala was stopped at Woodlark Island on the Strickland River and from that point on the supplies and equipment were moved forward by carrier relays, one-third in each relay. It took eighteen days to travel the 45 miles to the junction of the Rentoul and the Strickland Rivers. The expedition followed the Rentoul River and on the 18th of February they found the Rentoul River so blocked that from there on travelling was all on foot. In forty days they had travelled 84 miles and moved eight tons of supplies and equipment. They had named O'Malley's Peak and the Karius Mountains.

Three of the canoes were burnt and one canoe returned to Daru with four policemen and two sick carriers.

From the 14th of March when they were half way across the plateau the problems that had been anticipated began to emerge. One was the refusal of the local villagers to trade despite their large and well stocked gardens. The other was the hostility of the locals who began to appear in large numbers with occasional ambushes. Before the party reached the 'barrier' in early April Hides and constable Euwsi shot one of two villagers who had attempted to ambush them.

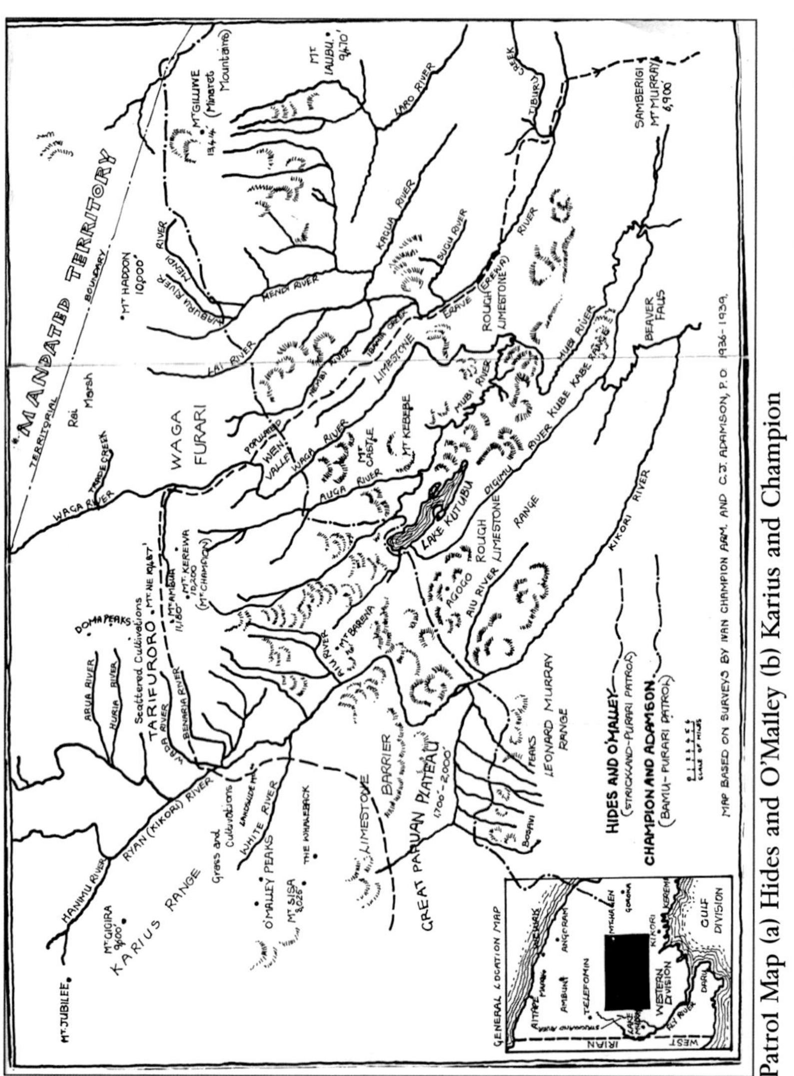

Patrol Map (a) Hides and O'Malley (b) Karius and Champion

Source: James Sinclair

On the 15th of April they reached a headwaters river of the Kikori River that they named the Ryan River. Here they were travelling in forest country and came upon great gardens and hundreds of villagers who still refused to trade.

It was decided to leave the area by rafting down the Purari River and before the four rafts were completed there were further clashes and more villagers were shot.In one incident six were killed.

On one occasion before they descended into the Waga Furari a thousand 'wigmen' put on a threatening show of chanting and yodelling. With the continuing refusal to trade the explorers resorted to raiding the gardens for food and leaving tomahawks as payment.

They were shown the Erave river a tributary and their path to the Purari River but had to survive a dangerous flooding of the chasm of the Iehi River. Soon after they received supplies of village sago, wild pig and cassowary to overcome the food problem. They reached the Ogomobu plantation (two hours from Kikori) on the 17th of June 1935, five months and 18 days after leaving Daru.

In total they had killed 32 villagers and Hides insisted that an enquiry be held immediately at Kikori. Humphries the local Magistrate conducted the enquiry that eventually cleared Hides and O'Malley. The enquiry disclosed that they had opened fire on nine occasions,five times to repel attacks and on four occasions to stop incipient attacks at close quarters.

In 1937 Hides led a horror expedition up the Fly River that he had to abandon. His partner Lyall became seriously ill and the carriers were stricken with a severe form of what Hides said was beri beri. Five of the carriers died and Hides decided to make a dash by raft down the river with Lyall. They set off on the 1st of September and made 70 miles on the first day .

On the second day Hides got a small dugout canoe and after travelling by day and by night they reached Totoma on the 6th of September. At midnight they ran into a tidal *bore* and they lost the canoe and all its contents. Hides made a raft and slowly travelled downstream. Hides assistant Biej walked the 65 miles along the western bank of the river in seven days to meet the Pauline. The Pauline took Lyall to Daru but unfortunately he did not recover from his illness.

Hides and O'Malley did not do any real survey or exploration of the Fly River but it was their access into the Papuan hinterland as it was with other expeditions that gave the world an understanding of what this part of New Guinea was like and who were the people who lived there.

The surveys by Captain Baker of the Fly River, the Omati River and the Kikori River increased the navigation knowledge about these streams in the interest of their future commercial use. This valuable work surely warrants his inclusion on the list of ships' captains who have applied their skills as hydrographers, navigators and explorers on the Fly River, and the rivers mentioned in this book just as M.V. Tiveri is truly entitled to be on record with HMS *Fly*,

Ellengowan, Neva, Bonito Merrie England, Elevala and those other vessels used by these men on their expeditions.

Schedule of Ships and Masters On Fly River Expeditions

Ship	Photo	Crew	Date
HMS *Fly*	58	Captain Francis Blackwood, Lt Yule, Lt Aird	1845
Ellengowan	99	Rev.Macfarlane, Luigi D'Albertis, H.M.Chester	1875
Neva	100	Luigi D'Albertis, Lawrence Hargrave	1876
Neva	100	D'Albertis, Preston	1877
S.S. Benito	102	Captain Henry Everill, John Douglas	1885
Merrie England	109	Sir William MacGregor, Cameron	1889/90
Laurabada	68	Sir Hubert Murray	1914 et al
Minnetonka	103	Leo Austin	1922 & 1924
Kismet	n/a	Sir Rupert Clarke and the Pryke brothers	1924
Elevala	103	Charles Karius	1926
Elevala	103	Charles Karius and Ivan Champion	1927
Laurabada	68	Jack Hides and James O'Malley	1935
Robin S, Peter Pan	n/a	Jack Hides and David Lyall	1937

Ship	Photo	Crew	Date
Tiveri	52	Captain E.H.B. Baker	1954
Contemporary PNG Expeditions not associated with the Fly River			
HMS *Bramble*		Lieutenant Yule	1845
HMS *Rattlesnake*		Captain Owen Stanley	1849
HMS *Basilisk*		Captain John Moresby	1871
S.S. *Chevert*		Mr John MacLeay	1875

Bibliography

Australian Dictionary of Biography, Vol. 4, (MUP), 1972.

Australian Dictionary of Biography, Vol. 5, (MUP), 1974.

Australian Dictionary of Biography, Vol. 7, (MUP), 2007.

Australian Dictionary of Biography, Vol. 8, (MUP), 1981.

Australian Dictionary of Biography, Vol. 10, (MUP), 1986.

Bauerlen, W, *The Voyage of the Bonito*, Gibbs Shellard & Co., Sydney, 1886.

Champion, Ivan, *Across New Guinea from the Fly to the Sepik,* Constable, U.K. 1932.

Clune, Frank, *Prowling Through Papua,* Angus and Robinson, Sydney, 1943.

Crawford, L.A., AIDA, Crawford Home Publishers

Everill, H.C., *Official Report,* New Guinea Expedition, Australian Geographic Society

Goode, John, *Rape of the Fly Exploration in New Guinea,* Nelson, Melbourne, 1977.

Hides and O'Malley, *The Strickland Purari Patrol,* 1934-36.

Royal Geographical Society of Australasia (Queensland), *Proceedings and transactions of the Queensland Branch of the Royal Geographical Society of Australia 1889/90*, Watson Ferguson & Co., Brisbane Vol. V Parts 1 & 2.

Ryan, Cornelius, *A Bridge Too Far*, Simon and Schuster, New York, 1974.

Sinclair, James, *Mastamak*, Crawford Home Publishers.

Sinclair, James, *The Money Tree*, Crawford Home Publishers.

Sinclair, James, *The Outside Man*, Lansdowne Press, 1960

The Canberra Times, December 1929.

The Courier Mail, Brisbane, 2 April 1890.

The Queenslander, 28 November 1885.

Wilkinson, Rick, *A Thirst For Burning*, David Ell Press, 1983 & 1988

Wilkinson, Rick, *Where God Never Trod*, David Ell Press, 1991.

Wilson, P.D., *Henry M. Chester's report of the Ellengowan voyage up the Fly River.*